SEEKING the
HIDDEN GOD

*S*EEKING the *H*IDDEN *G*OD

Jane Kopas

ORBIS BOOKS
Maryknoll, New York 10545

Founded in 1970, Orbis Books endeavors to publish works that enlighten the mind, nourish the spirit, and challenge the conscience. The publishing arm of the Maryknoll Fathers and Brothers, Orbis seeks to explore the global dimensions of the Christian faith and mission, to invite dialogue with diverse cultures and religious traditions, and to serve the cause of reconciliation and peace. The books published reflect the views of their authors and do not represent the official position of the Maryknoll Society. To learn more about Maryknoll and Orbis Books, please visit our website at www.maryknoll.org.

Published by Orbis Books, Maryknoll, New York 10545-0308.
Manufactured in the United States of America.

Library of Congress Cataloging-in-Publication Data

Kopas, Jane.
    Seeking the hidden God / Jane Kopas.
      p. cm.
    Includes index.
    ISBN-13: 978-1-57075-624-5 (pbk.)
    1. Hidden God. 2. Bible—Evidences, authority, etc. 3. Spiritual life—Christianity. I. Title.
    BT180.H54K58 2005
    231—dc22
                                     2005009080

Contents

Part III
Cultivating Spiritual Skills

Preface

This book aims to address the need for a spirituality that takes the hiddenness of God seriously. It is not a treatise on God. The quest for a vision of a spirituality of hiddenness and the strength to work it out is not new. It has roots in the long history of spiritual seekers. But while it is not new, it has special relevance in our age, which does not deal well with what is hidden. I hope others will find my exploration helpful as they make their own path into unknown territory. I hope they, too, will find challenging and encouraging companions on the journey.

In writing this book I have been helped by the comments, suggestions, and encouragement of friends and co-seekers, some of whom read drafts and some parts of the book. These include Elaine Bane who read several drafts as the work evolved, the late Ruth Brennan, Kathleen Fischer, Mary Anne Foley, Sandra Schneiders, Gertrude Wilkinson, and colleagues in the Department of Theology at the University of Scranton. I also thank Susan Perry of Orbis for her editorial guidance and the University of Scranton for a sabbatical and other time to pursue this project.

I

Recovering the
Tradition of a
Hidden God

≈

1

The "Disappearing" God

Thomas Merton captured the imagination of his generation with *Seven Storey Mountain*, an autobiographical account of his conversion to Catholicism and entrance into the Trappist monastery of Gethsemani in Kentucky. Many readers in the late 1940s were intrigued by the notion that an urbane, self-centered intellectual found belief in God so compelling that he would leave a stimulating worldly life for a silent life with God. Barely twenty years after writing the book, however, the monk was no longer writing of God with the glow of a recent convert's discovery of God; he was writing instead of the hidden and elusive God.

Merton observed in the late 1960s that it is not unusual for modern people, even faithful believers, to experience all sorts of difficulty with belief in God.[1] "It is more and more usual for modern people to be afflicted with a sense of absence, desolation, and incapacity to even 'want' to pray or think about God," he says. This "disappearance" of God presents people today with an unprecedented challenge.

It was apparent to Merton that it is no longer only philosophers and avowed atheists in smoke-filled cafés who think about the absence of God. Now, the topic has filtered down to the general public. Even ordinary believers willingly admit that they no longer know God as they once thought they did. Numerous writers confirm this experience as they speak of the absence of God, the death of God, the eclipse of God, the hiddenness of God. It is evident that Merton understood the challenge facing those who believe but who need help with their unbelief.

At a crossroads of faith, believers may turn toward the easy paths of cynicism or secure religion. If they become cynical, they are tempted to view whatever is religious with an attitude of suspicion. Religious tradition may appear as little more than a relic of the unscientific past and a tool of those seeking spiritual power. If cynics concede that religion still has any value, they tend to see it as a crutch to comfort those who are not strong enough or independent enough to face life's hard realities. Cynics find themselves more at home in a world of disillusionment than in a world whose spiritual dimensions are hidden.

Others, whose idealized view of religion still survives, may look for a secure religious outlook that offers stable truths and the promise of answers. They may look for a church based on a literal reading of the Bible, or for a faith community that validates their suspicion of secular culture. Whoever can promise *answers* to their nagging questions and sense of isolation will get a sympathetic hearing.

Neither of these approaches will prepare a person to discover a hidden God in the midst of contemporary life. For those who trust that God's truth can be hidden in strange places, another way is needed. It is the more difficult path of spiritual wisdom, full of a mixture of multiplicity and change as well as sacred truth.

Those who seek the path of wisdom are much less likely to be disheartened by the failures of religion to meet expectations. They will see religious beliefs and practices as part of a map that helps on some stretches of the journey with God but not on others. They will not view the map as an end in itself. At some point it will become apparent to the seeker of wisdom that God cannot be contained in any formula, no matter how lofty. They find themselves learning to live with a measure of ambiguity and uncertainty, guided by a trust that the heart will learn what it really needs to know about God. A contemplative attitude appears to be their best guide.

Many factors bring people to this crossroads today where God seems more hidden than ever before. Among these factors is the realization that the religious, theological, and cultural world that supported our understanding of God in the past no longer offers the same support it once did. Analyzing causes of the demise of a cohesive religious world view won't necessarily restore us to a trouble-free faith. Analysis keeps us focused on intellectual knowledge that touches only one aspect of faith in God. The mystery of a hidden God is the mystery of relationship itself. But it can still be useful to consider intellectual aspects of the modern phenomenon. This inquiry will allow us to gain a fuller sense of how the disappearance of certain beliefs can affect our sense of the presence of God.

A God beyond Mere Ideas

People may protest that belief in God is not disappearing. They will cite evidence like the Gallup poll of the Princeton Religious Research Center that revealed that 97 percent of Americans surveyed believe in God or a universal spirit.[2] But this finding, published in 1996, doesn't tell us whether the God people believe in now is the one they have always believed in. In fact, an earlier survey indicated that more than 80 percent of those surveyed felt that individuals should arrive at their own religious beliefs without conformity to those of a church or synagogue.

This assertion of independent belief suggests the respondents had already arrived at ideas that do not conform perfectly to those of their religious institutions. It appears that many people quietly shift their ideas of God as they make their way through their own unique life experiences. The way people have thought about God in the past is not necessarily the way they think about God today.

Both ideas and feelings about God are affected by the changing culture we live in. Most of us have come to accept the inevitability of change, even in something as stable as religion. Accepting change doesn't mean it will be comfortable or that it will lead immediately to positive new ideas. Until we find a way to integrate faith and experience in a changing world, we may have to endure spiritual discomfort. That discomfort can feel very much like the disappearance of God.

From conversations with many others and from my own reflection, I detect a vague sense of spiritual discomfort. I hear people say, "I don't know what I believe about God now." Ideas that were formerly unquestioned appear to be losing some of their power. This gives the impression of a "disappearing" God, or an elusive God who no longer conforms to familiar traditional beliefs.

The God who is disappearing is the authoritarian God of authoritarian religion. Previous generations were taught to look to the Bible or the church to inform them of correct belief. They were given clear guidelines of what God expected and what constituted sin when they did not live up to divine expectations. Doubt was unacceptable. Questioning was dangerous. This no longer seems to be the case.

The God who is disappearing is the God who created the world complete from the beginning, establishing every species and a perfect first human couple. With every aspect of creation coming from the hand of God, we expected nothing new under the sun. Nor did we expect there was any role for human beings in creation except to praise God and to be responsible stewards of a creation that was essentially complete. Both the evidence of evolution and the potential of technology contradict this view.

The God who is disappearing is the God who allows evils to occur because they are designed to bring about some greater good. Even if these evils were thought to occur because of natural disasters or as a result of the free will of human beings, there was somehow an inscrutable divine purpose that allowed evils to occur. Whatever the explanation for evil, God was seen as always foreseeing and allowing what happens. Some people today question whether God created a world under this kind of divine control.

The God who is disappearing is the God who decided Jesus must die in order for others to be saved. This God required that restitution be made for the primal sin of human beings that disrupted the harmony of the world. Since the offense was committed by human beings, it had to be compensated for by a human being; since it offended the infinite God, it had to be compensated for by one who had the status of God. The God of Absolute Justice settles for nothing less than the sacrifice of the Son. Some question whether God really demands this kind of justice, or whether it simply reflects a human thirst for absolute justice.

The God who is disappearing is the God who is "male," the God who is revealed primarily through masculine images, pronouns, or activities. This God exercises a particular kind of power and until recently chooses only representatives like "himself." In some Christian communities the official representatives of God may be black or white, healthy or disabled, old or young, but still not female. Changes in social structures lead people to raise questions about this view of God.

For Catholic Christians like me, the God who is disappearing or has disappeared is the God who is revealed fully in only one religion, Catholic Christianity. This God wants all people to see the light of truth revealed exclusively in Jesus. Other religions might contain hints of religious truth, but it is found fully only in foundational Christianity. Doubt has been cast on this absolute position because it discounts the religious tradition and experience of a majority of the world's population. It also discounts the holiness of many saintly people those religious traditions have nurtured.

The God who is disappearing is the God who had one definite purpose in life for each person; whether it was to be marriage to a particular person, a fruitful single life, or a consecrated religious life. Given this belief, God's plan could not be thwarted without great unhappiness. All one had to do was to learn God's will, which would, of course, remain untouched by new situations that came along. The pervasiveness of change and the value of personal responsibility make this view questionable.

There are many who still feel God's presence basically as they always have. In some cases they may have made adjustments in their understanding of God, but these have been smooth and untroubled. They do not feel that God is elusive.

There are also some whose understanding has changed so imperceptibly they may not be aware how much it has changed. They sense only vaguely that God is more hidden and elusive than they formerly thought.

But for others, the mystery of God so colors their relationship with God that they are intensely aware of darkness, hiddenness, or even absence while they still believe in God. For these, the "disappearance" of God is not a sign that God is no longer present because beliefs are less certain. Rather, the greater hiddenness of God holds an invitation to ponder the meaning of presence and absence in a new spiritual landscape where faith takes on a new meaning.

To speak of a "disappearing" God is not to suggest that God does not exist. When something "disappears," it is no longer evident through its former appearance, but it can still be present. After a rain, water is evident, but before long it disappears. It takes on a different form of presence in the atmosphere. Because the water no longer appears in its original form does not mean it can't manifest itself in another way. Perceiving other forms of presence, however, does require us to loosen our dependence on just one way of identifying presence and absence such as through beliefs.

As we try to plumb the mystery of the hidden God, we may rely too heavily on beliefs. Beliefs have a tendency to become the most familiar way to call God to mind. We can become so accustomed to judging the presence of God by our ability to feel or to think of God in particular ideas, words, or beliefs, that we easily miss more subtle forms of presence.

We would do well to get past the tendency to equate faith, which can be inarticulate, with belief, which depends on ideas. Faith is the irreducible ground of our trust in God; beliefs are the verbal expressions of the ideas that anchor our trust. Beliefs and ideas are important, but they alone do not express God's presence or absence.

All ideas are limited, especially ideas of God. Once we try to put God into words, we compress God into a manageable expression. God cannot be managed in this way.

At the same time, we can't dispense with ideas about God entirely because they help us to express faith and to deal with obstacles to faith. There are times when the intellect and imagination are crucial in the preservation of faith; and there are also times when they must take a back seat to the more subtle senses that guide us as we probe the mystery of a hidden God.

Probing the Mystery of a Hidden God

While the search for an elusive God may not be an intellectual project, we need to be ready to call reason into its service. The intellect is needed when faith becomes problematic, and we need to know whether to defend, reinterpret, or discard the beliefs that have supported it. The intellect is needed when our religious heritage seems to suggest a single voice for speaking of God, and we suspect there are other voices that have been neglected. The intellect is needed when dominant ideas threaten to block openness to deeper spiritual truths. As some of the ideas of a "disappearing" God suggest, the way we think can affect the way we respond to divinity. Take, for example, the weight we now give to the influence of science and the societal status of women on our images and ideas of God. When the idea of evolution took hold of the modern imagination, believers had to deal with their feelings about God's power in creation. Was that power something that overrode all other forms of power, or could creation include the possibility of species evolving and human beings sharing in creative power?

The question believers faced was not simply whether God had power or not, but what kind of power could be imagined. From the point of view of the Bible, the issue at stake is whether to hold to a literal interpretation of God's creation of the world in Genesis, or to accept a less literal understanding of God's role in creation. Many came to believe that a less literal understanding of the creation account could lead to a deeper understanding of God's power and could make it possible to embrace the insights of the biblical tradition while at the same time accepting the idea of evolution. For them, it is not necessary to retreat to a religious ghetto of fundamentalism to guard against the dangers of new scientific insights.

A similar challenge to ideas of God arises from a critique of the masculine bias of Christian tradition. The fatherhood of God and the sonship of Christ, taken as exclusive images of God, could lead to idolatry. The transcendence of God could be lost if Christians failed to look for a God beyond gender. Contemporary religious thinkers have probed the intellectual tradition of Christianity and uncovered traditions that insist on a hidden Spirit of God and a Jesus who liberates believers from patriarchal structures. The uncovering of alternative resources demonstrates that a religious heritage may be more inclusive than it first appears.

As important as these issues are, intellectual challenges are only one part of a bigger picture. Intellectual challenges ought to be dealt with, but they do not define a relationship with God. When we open ourselves to the mystery of a relationship with God, when we seek to know God more intimately, we are led beyond the borders of familiar concepts. Life in relationship does not depend exclusively on our ego-directed ability to find the right words and ideas. Both religious traditions and the individuals who question them ought not forget a critical truth: faith is wider and deeper than belief.

The poet Denise Levertov, who became agnostic after a religious childhood, struggled for years with questions of belief and the problem of suffering. Eventually, she re-embraced her Christian heritage, but she did not recover faith either through reasoning or through a dramatic personal conversion. She found it by surrendering to a relationship.

Levertov traces her return to faith to a period when she was working on a poem structured on the framework of the Mass. By the time she arrived at the Agnus Dei she noticed a change in her attitude toward the material. She felt herself moved by something other than intellectual assent, but faith was not fully evident. Slowly, she began to realize she could not resolve her questions through her own reasoning or theology. She had to live her way into faith instead of waiting until she was convinced that she could make sense of it. She had to lean back into her relationship with God, who was hidden.

The God she was coming to accept was elusive, but she realized she was also elusive. In a poem called "Flickering Mind," Levertov imagines herself as a minnow, attracted by God's presence but constantly darting away into the shadows.[3] She cannot hold her self still. She asks how she can focus her flickering, to make contact with a presence she cannot perceive clearly.

The poem is a study in the ripening of a relationship with God. Levertov admits she has overcome her reluctance to speak of God and has grown to a point where she can look honestly at her own limits, but her search to know God is limited by her mind's capacity to sustain attention. She accepts her limits and yearns to transcend them. She is driven now, not by her need for answers but by a question, "How can I focus my flickering?" The question does not lead to a clear answer but rather to the discovery of a relationship so basic, so personal and existential, that it transcends words. Only after the ideas, images, and theologies have taken seekers to the edge, do they find themselves in the presence of the mystery that cannot be captured in words. Thinking about God takes us only so far.

The Sufi poet Rumi, who remained faithful to Islam while he stretched its boundaries, writes of the failure of all words to contain the infinite God. His poetry paradoxically sought to capture a fuller experience of God in words, while questioning the ability of language to express the experience. Words are like jars of water that contain only a small part of a vast body of water, he says.[4] At some point these jars of spring water are not enough anymore, and so Rumi begs, "take us down to the river."

God is the river we seek, but we may be wary about how far we can enter its depths. We sometimes approach the mystery of God through theological ideas that will remove obstacles to faith and communicate the meaning of God. This approach takes us only into shallow water. As we enter deeper waters of the silent God, ideas are less important.

If our faith is true and deepening, it will urge us into the trackless waters of the silence of God where muted sounds and subtle currents can be dimly discerned. There faith will take us toward the channels of the river where we may hear a new song—or hear an old song in a new way.

Those of us who grew up within a religious tradition learned the familiar ideas and images of that tradition, its particular words of belief and praise, so we usually think we know the song well. Yet, it is possible to learn the words without developing an ear for the music that carries us into the currents of the river of God. Words allow us to converse with other mortals, but having an ear for music allows us to listen to God who communicates without words. To hear the spiritual sounds beneath religious doctrines, we need the ability to listen for faint music.

God has become elusive for some of us, not because we haven't figured out the right technique for tracking, not because God is capricious, and not because God is punishing us for failing to be faithful enough, but because we are in a different place where old explanations don't capture the relationship. We cannot speak of the relationship as we once did. We cannot control it, just as we cannot control other important relationships. We need to learn to wait and observe. Certain ways of understanding God are disappearing, so God seems to elude us. But we can discover God, even in apparent absence, if we are willing to be found in the dark.

Exploring a Darker Path

Some find themselves drawn to this topic because, despite years of faithful devotion to God, their changing ideas of God and changing relationship to God have brought them to a place they never anticipated. They wonder what brought them to this strange spot. They ask how others have dealt with this situation as they look for guidance. I have wondered and asked these questions, too. This book is my attempt to share what I am learning.

I am not writing this book for those who are content with the faith and formulas that introduced them to God, or for those whose religious practices have taken them to the God they expected. I accept and respect the faith that is supported by their experience. But the experience others have of religious diversity, their awareness of physical and social sciences, the development of their personal religious thought, and their evolving desire for God in a new context—all require a different approach to God. I am writing this book for those who, like me, find themselves in a place where they are convinced that God is present but are not sure how to speak of or deal with a presence that seems more elusive than before. I am writing it for those who also suspect it is they, not God, who have become more elusive.

I do not think this experience is uncommon. Nor do I believe that it must be a negative experience. On the contrary, the experience of an elusive God is a moment of truth and liberation from some of the ideas of God that limit faith. The experience opens new possibilities for knowing God and ourselves.

This book is an attempt to get beyond hesitation to speak about a God who seems to have disappeared. It reflects the implausible desire to speak about a God who cannot be spoken about, to affirm a presence that calls us, through the experience of absence, to an adventure of the spirit.

The first part of this book focuses on recovering the tradition of an elusive God. People today often feel they are experiencing a modern or post-modern phenomenon that has arisen purely because we live in an age of spiritual uncertainty. We do live in such an age, and we need to recognize how pluralism, technology, and the information explosion have converged to change how we see things. But that does not tell the whole story.

God has been recognized as elusive since biblical times. Both the Hebrew Scriptures and the Christian Scriptures caution against the tendency to equate God with our ideas of God. Christian theologians who spoke of the way of negation did so to remind their listeners that the God we do not know is truer than the God we think we know. The mystics embraced a dark night of yearning for God because they realized that the God they sought could only be found in a cloud of unknowing. For the sake of a mature spirituality we, too, need to accept the mystery of God's elusive presence without running from the challenge it represents.

The second part of the book deals with the need to use ideas and images that will preserve the hiddenness of God. It recognizes a shift from hierarchical and unchanging images of God to other kinds of relational images; however, the relational images we use should not be simple one-dimensional images that suggest one kind of presence. The hidden presence of God cannot be so simply objectified. To speak of a hidden God at all, we need images multi-faceted enough to allow God to remain hidden.

Paradoxical images, like challenging companion, compassionate adversary, and fertile emptiness, help us to recognize that every image conceals as well as reveals. These multi-dimensional images help to lessen our tendency to try to pin God down. They preserve a paradoxical tension. Becoming at home with the "sometimes this way" and "sometimes that way" of relationships allows us to pick up clues to the positive value of elusiveness.

The third part of the book explores conditions that challenge our ability to stay aware of the hidden God, and it identifies skills needed to meet the challenge. The spiritual skills that guided our traditional religious life are still valuable, but new skills need to be cultivated in order to deal with today's situation. Because we live in an age that tempts us to the wrong kinds of passivity and biases us toward certain kinds of action, we cannot simply rely on the virtues that fit another age.

In an age of pluralism we need to learn how to be rooted in a religious tradition while remaining open to God's presence in other religious traditions. In an age of technology and multi-tasking, we need to cultivate the spirit of contemplation that allows us to understand our real limits and to see grace in the ordinary. In an age of information and pragmatism, we need to cultivate radical self-knowledge that flows from spiritual wisdom instead of settling for the kind of knowledge that comes from self-help manuals.

In every age and for every person, situations change and new spiritual skills are needed. Well into his religious life, Thomas Merton was still learning about himself and the ways of God. He realized, in time, that he didn't need to escape the secular world to find God or attain holiness; he came to believe, instead, that he had to get a new perspective on it. He also learned just how much his ideas of God and self still needed to be purified. He found himself exploring a darker path. Merton's prayer reveals how much he didn't understand about himself or God:

> My Lord God, I have no idea where I am going. I do not see the road ahead of me. I cannot know for certain where it will end. Nor do I really know myself, and the fact that I think I am following your will does not mean I am actually doing so. But I believe that the desire to please you does in fact please you.[5]

Early in his spiritual life, through his reading of *The Spirit of Medieval Philosophy* by Etienne Gilson, Merton had discovered a new concept of God as Being itself, a concept more expansive than the oversized humanized version he had previously imagined and rejected.[6] As he lived out his commitment, he discovered just how unfathomable that God is. Merton came to address God as one whose infinite light is darkness to him, whose immensity is as the void to him.[7]

Maybe that is why he responded compassionately to those who felt that God was no longer present in familiar ways. He wanted to assure them that their experience was not a situation to be lamented. For Merton, feelings of presence and absence are to be expected in a relationship with God. God's presence to the world (and each of us) is unlimited; our presence to God is limited. Once we come to a better grasp of the contrast between God and ourselves, it will not be surprising that feelings of both presence and absence are part of the relationship.

Merton felt that the way a person approaches the situation will affect his or her ability to learn from it. Ignoring or fleeing from the feeling of absence will not relieve the distress or resolve the doubt. It continues to nag. Reverting to the trouble-free faith of an earlier stage won't work either. To settle for the faith that once expressed a relationship would be to miss an opportunity to deepen faith. Spiritual growth doesn't happen when we try to ignore challenges or hold on to the past.

Instead of lamenting the apparent loss of an earlier faith, or resorting to methods of preserving it that are more appropriate to another time, the person who feels the absence of God should see it as an opportunity. Merton believes that person is being called to move to a new level of prayer and meditation, one that better fits the person's present stage of spiritual life and relationship with God.

Reading, reflection, and prayer helped Merton to broaden and deepen his spiritual outlook. He also broadened his outlook by corresponding and conversing with a diverse collection of people. And, it goes without saying, he learned from the writings and lives of spiritual guides who preceded him. Like him, we, too, can find insight and encouragement in many places. Consulting our spiritual ancestors, who walked an unfamiliar path with a hidden God, is a good place to start.

2

The Elusive God of Hebrew Scriptures

Our first spiritual ancestors, men and women of the Bible, seem to have experienced God more vividly and directly than we do. From Adam and Eve in the garden to Moses at the burning bush to Jonah in the belly of the whale, the presence they encountered appears unmistakable. When we read of these encounters, we can easily assume our predecessors had a clear idea of who God is. A closer look at the Bible suggests otherwise.[1]

The great heroes of Israel, and the communities that preserved their stories, often found they did not understand God as well as they thought they did. They had to continue to exercise faith even though they had an intimate relationship with God. The dilemmas that arose from their encounters with the God of mystery were not driven by theoretical questions but were led by continuing challenges. These challenges made them ponder who God is, the meaning of suffering, and their relation to other religions. They learned again and again that they should not take their understanding of God for granted.

The challenge of trying to understand a relationship with God involves more than simply holding on to a faith rooted in foundational events. Foundational events turn our attention to the past. While it is important to remember past encounters with God, we cannot expect that we will always meet God in the same way. God confounds habitual expectations and conventional understanding. Our spiritual ancestors persisted in struggling to comprehend the God who called them, but they were sometimes blind to the narrowness of their expectations. When they expected God to be present in a particular way, the people often learned how little they knew God.

The Bible makes a point of letting the reader know that God does not "think" or "act" according to our expectations. In fact, an unsettling undercurrent—a subversive tradition—runs through the Bible. The sacred writings that confidently tell us about God's presence in history can also subvert or undermine our simplistic ways of thinking of that presence.

The presence of God among people is not always what one would expect, both because God is mystery and because we live in a world of change. Conditions change, people change, and in some situations God seems to change. The God of the Israelites is a living God, fostering dynamic relationships. This is a God who takes the people into new places where the old answers may not fit. When old answers do not fit and people no longer know what to expect, they find God to be elusive.

The Hebrew Scriptures offer powerful examples of a God of mystery who both unsettles and liberates. This tradition of a disconcerting God runs like a contrasting thread through a number of books of the Bible. The tradition of subversion, often neglected, is full of suggestions of a hidden God. The long history of this phenomenon becomes evident when we consider some of the Hebrew Bible's subversive challenges to faith in God, challenges such as suffering, transformation, expansive love, and intimacy.

The Challenge of Suffering

The story of Job contributes to the hidden tradition of the ever-present but elusive God. Job was a devoted servant of God who enjoyed what were regarded as the God-given rewards of being a good person. He had a large family, good health, and many material blessings. God knew him to be faithful and treated him accordingly. But, as the story goes, a tempter suggests that God should test Job to see if he is faithful only in good times. God goes along with the suggestion and takes away Job's family, his possessions, and his health.

Job's friends come to "console" him. They try to help him by analyzing why he is suffering. Each of his friends offers an analysis of his situation based on the theology of suffering that prevailed at that time. This theology was rooted in a belief that all suffering is punishment for sin. If you suffered, you had sinned and were reaping the punishment. His friends admonished Job to confess his guilt before God and to repent so that God would restore him to favor. But Job had not sinned. He knew from his own experience that this theology was no longer convincing. Whether it worked in the past or not, it wasn't effective in explaining how God operated in his case.

Job defends himself, perplexed as to why he has been afflicted with so much suffering. Strangely, God does not respond to Job even to reveal that Job was being tested. Instead, God offers a series of questions Job cannot answer. "Where were you when I laid the foundation of the earth?" "Do you know the ordinances of the heavens?" "Do you give the horse its might?" God makes no attempt to explain "why" Job suffered. God's response in the Book of Job subverts the old theology of suffering as a punishment for sin, but it also subverts the notion that there is a logical explanation for everything. In place of a coherent theology, we meet a God beyond understanding.

Job admits that God is too much for him, and he will go no further. But God continues to speak of the wonders of creation and the divine role in it until finally Job answers that he now realizes God can do all things. He no longer has to question or understand because he experientially knows his relationship to the all-wise and powerful God. He accepts the inscrutable mystery of God saying, "now my eye sees you," instead of taking the word of others as he did before.

At several points in the story, we get the impression of an arbitrary and non-listening God, a God who does not express concern for human suffering. But this impression comes from focusing too much on one part of the story. A longer view reveals God's abiding concern about relationships. We must stay with the story until its end to understand the relational challenge of suffering and God's compassion.

At the end of the story God chastises Job's friends because they have not spoken rightly as Job has. They are to go to Job and offer sacrifice. Job is commanded to pray for them. When Job has prayed for his friends, God restores his fortunes twofold. Nothing is said about why the suffering came about or how it should have been handled. What seems more important is how Job and his friends handle their relationship with one another.

God's role in restoring harmony and justice seems puzzling. If God were really as annoyed with Job's questioning as it seems, why would God restore Job's fortunes not just to what they were before but to twice as much? If Job admitted once that he had overstepped his bounds in questioning God, why wasn't his first admission sufficient? And why did he have to pray for his friends?

Both Job and his friends had lessons to learn. Job had to learn compassion and forgiveness of his friends by praying for them instead of resenting them. The friends, who are an essential part of the story, had to learn the futility of trying to find logical reasons for suffering. Reading the story with an eye toward its final resolution can draw us deeper into the mystery of God and the limits of reason. Within this mystery, we can see the importance of not fixating on suffering or ourselves, but on learning how to respond to suffering and to attempts to explain it.

The Book of Job disturbs the reader profoundly. But it sometimes disturbs us for the wrong reasons. On one level it disturbs us because it does not provide a justification for suffering. It doesn't explain that there is a reason for everything that happens. Would suffering be any more acceptable if it always made sense? It also may disturb us because we see it as an example of the suffering of an innocent person. Would it be easier to justify suffering if we could categorize those who deserve it and those who do not? These concerns may be understandable, but the Book of Job should disturb us differently.

The Book of Job should disturb us not only because it exposes the limits of logic when it comes to suffering. It should disturb us because it shows how easily we get trapped by our desire to avoid all ills. This avoidance distracts us from learning to deal with the suffering we will inevitably encounter. Even more important, the Book of Job should challenge us because it invites us to look not only at the causes of suffering but also at the humanizing way we might respond to it. The book invites us to wonder what is being asked of those who suffer and those who care for them in a world where suffering cannot be avoided. It even suggests we should pray for those who try too hard to explain it.

If God had answered Job's questions to his satisfaction, he and we would have an acceptable rational God. We would never have to change or adjust to new situations. We would never have to wrestle with God or wonder whether we were caught in the trap of our own ideas of God. We would fail to encounter the Holy One who transforms us as we are always transformed, by entering into relationships that stretch us in hidden ways, not simply by having our questions answered.

The conclusion of Job's story does not show God offering a better theology of suffering than that posed by Job's friends. It's likely there is no convincing theology of suffering, maybe not a wholly convincing theology of God either. Theologies are not a substitute for living faith, even though they can help us at times. The Book of Job seeks to quiet the desperate need to know "why." Even when we seem to find acceptable reasons, knowing them may not make us better believers. Seeking reasons too vigorously may even get in the way of our transformation.

The Challenge of Surrender to Transformation

Job's encounter with God is not the only place in the Bible where we see ideas of God subverted. We find another prime example in Moses. Moses lived in the thirteenth century B.C.E., a time when people believed in many gods.

While tending the flocks one day, Moses spotted a strange phenomenon, a bush that continued to burn without being consumed. As he moved toward it in fascination, he heard a voice that warned him he was on holy ground and needed to remove his sandals. In the extended conversation that followed, God revealed a destiny for Moses. He was to return to Egypt as God's emissary and to be an instrument in God's liberation of the people of Israel. Moses did what any sensible person would do. He tried to get out of the job.

Among the strategies Moses used to avoid going to Egypt was to question God's identity since the voice he perceived could have been that of any of a number of gods. No doubt, Moses cared about knowing God's identity. But given his other arguments to escape the task he was being given, he seemed at first to be more interested in finding a way to manage his relations with this God.

The only gods that Moses knew were the gods his predecessors and contemporaries celebrated. So which of these was the God who spoke to him? If he knew God's identity, he would know what to expect and how to deal with God. If he knew the way God dealt with human beings, he could calculate the path that would put him a step ahead of God. He could invoke God's name and gain control over his own destiny. He could add this God to the pantheon of divinities to bargain with and appease.

The God who confronted Moses was not about to become another household deity. When Moses asks what he should say when asked who sent him, God subverts Moses' expectations and resists domestication by answering, "I will be who I will be." It is a name more mysterious than Moses could imagine. By revealing this name, God assures Moses that the divine presence will be with him but does not reveal in advance in what form it will appear to support or challenge him. Moses could not know from the basic contours of God's "plan" that one of the most important consequences of following God's direction would be the formation of a new identity and new self-understanding for Moses and for the Israelite community.

Most of Moses' objections to God's request revolved around his self-perception. First, he objected that the Israelites would not believe him. Then he said he was not a skilled speaker. Finally, he simply asked God to send someone else. At this early stage of his relationship with God, Moses was interested mainly in saving himself and preserving his limited control; if he was interested in God or the suffering Israelites, he could not fathom the implications of entering into these relationships that would transform him.

Moses finally yielded to God and went to Egypt to do God's bidding. He let go of the idea that there were certain things he had to know beforehand. His insecurity was eventually replaced with a confidence in God that gave him courage to respond wholeheartedly to God's call. He even learned to "argue" with God at a more honest level. As Moses threw himself into the task God gave him—relentlessly admonishing the pharaoh, leading the people, rebuking them for their idolatry—his own identity was reshaped by his relationship with God. In the process Moses was stretched to great compassion for his people.

We see growth in Moses' relationship with God and with the people when God sends them out of Sinai. At first God refuses to go with them because of their obstinacy. But Moses pleads with God not to remove the divine presence. He cannot conceive of himself or his people without God. God relents and promises to stay with Moses and the people. God also answers Moses' request to see the divine glory, but only if he hides in the cleft of a rock and only from the "back" as God passes. Moses gets another lesson in accepting the hidden God.

In the years before and after the Exodus, Moses would find himself in circumstances that did not yield the immediate results he, or we, might expect. The Egyptians did not respond to multiple warnings, and the Israelites were not spared from further suffering. After they were freed from Egypt, their Exodus did not lead immediately into the Promised Land. When the people finally stood on the threshold of the Promised Land, Moses knew he would not enter it with them. The greatest fulfillment of God's promise to him was found, not in a temporary achievement, but in his transformation, along with the other Israelites, into God's people.

We are led to believe that Job and Moses learned to come to a peace with God in the maturing of their faith. Whatever else they learned, they appear to have learned that the way they journeyed was just as important as the achievement of their goal. Not everyone learns that lesson. Sometimes self-righteousness gets in the way of discovering who God is.

The Challenge of Inclusive Love

The prophet Jonah was called by God to preach the need for repentance to the people of Nineveh. At the same time, his call turned out to be a summons for him to repent and grow in compassion. This irony offers another example of God's subverting the expectations of the prophet. Though Jonah is counted among the prophets, the style of the Book of Jonah is as much ironic as prophetic. Those who prefer to dismiss it because of its outrageous fish story miss the irony.

Jonah was a prophet sent by God to Nineveh to announce that the city would be destroyed because of its wicked ways. Knowing the dangers that faced prophets, he tried to escape his commission by taking a ship that was going in the opposite direction. God, determined that Jonah would go to Nineveh, caused a terrible storm to beset the boat. When the sailors ask who on board was responsible for God's wrath, Jonah confesses that he is the one and tells them to throw him overboard so the storm will stop. And they do. And it does. Then Jonah is swallowed by a great fish, and, with no way out, he praises the powerful God and prays for deliverance. Once the fish spits him out, it is clear Jonah still has to fulfill his mission.

When Jonah gets to Nineveh, he goes through the city warning everyone that the city will be destroyed in forty days. All the people, including the king, listen and repent. So God spares the city. When Jonah sees that God has relented because the people took the message to heart, he is furious. Why should God be merciful to these people who were considered to be enemies of Israel?

The story can be understood only if we see it as a fable and understand the ideology it subverts. The book was most likely written after the Exile in Babylon. Before the Exile, the nation of Israel saw itself as a people favored by God and saw other nations as less worthy. This ideology was called into question at the end of the Exile when the Jews experienced the kindness of the benevolent non-Jewish leader Cyrus, who allowed them to go back to their homeland.

How were the Jews now to think of God since it was through the goodness of a non-Jew that they were liberated? How were they to relate to enemies who were not all enemies? The traditional Jewish belief that God set them apart as a holy people might need to be expanded. God could be hidden anywhere.

The prophet Jonah seems to be trying to hold on to an earlier experience of God as he insists on the preservation of Israel's religious purity and its exclusive claim on God's mercy. He maintains a position of religious superiority to the end. We do not know if Jonah ever repents and expands his vision, for the book ends with God reproving him for his failure to be compassionate. The message of God, which is directed to Jonah as well as to the Ninevites, eludes Jonah as he stubbornly insists on holding to his preconceptions about what God ought to do.

The Book of Jonah, one of the shortest of the prophetic books, does not leave us on first impression with the sense of a hidden God. Quite the opposite; it leaves us with a sense of God's bold action and Jonah's anger at it. It appears that Jonah understands what God is about. But Jonah doesn't really understand the mystery of God's inclusive love and his participation in that mystery. The true God is hidden from Jonah both because of his stubbornness and because God's compassion is boundless.

Jonah has missed the point, and he can't seem to journey farther in his relationship with God because what eludes him is the meaning of compassion. He wants God to follow his logic. He doesn't have a clue about the limits of his logic.

Jonah is a man of resentment. He resents being a prophet, resents having an assignment he doesn't agree with, resents God being merciful to people he doesn't like. He can't be happy if things don't turn out as he wants. Resentment constricts the flow of mercy. It limits the possibility of seeing a bigger picture. Resentment is the bitter fruit of self-righteousness, and self-righteousness stands in the way of an increasingly inclusive love. Resentment closes the door to the mystery of expansive love that is God.

The God of expansive love is the hidden God who ventures into strange places and invites us to follow. Jonah resisted the invitation and failed to appreciate the richness of a hidden God. The richness of the hidden God, the Hebrew Scriptures tell us, may also be discovered in a startling way in the mystery of intimacy with God.

The Challenge of Intimacy

We might be tempted to think that intimacy and hiddenness are mutually exclusive, but they are not. Intimacy can lead not only to better understanding but also to new depths of mystery in relation-

ships. The better we get to know another person, the more we realize and come to respect that they encompass a hidden world we cannot inhabit. No one's inner life is completely exposed to another.
Freedom of spirit dwells in the secret caverns of the heart where some
part of the other must always be absent from us.

This mystery is evident in the Song of Songs, a dramatic poem
describing a dialogue between two lovers. These are lovers for whom
desire and fulfillment create a tension that continually expands the
relationship, revealing there are depths that remain hidden.

The speaker in the Song of Songs praises the beauty of the
beloved, comparing the beloved to the most beautiful things in a
Middle Eastern pastoral setting—fine wine, fragrant oils, doves,
apple trees, gazelles. Their moments together are celebrated in the
erotic language of sensual satisfaction. And the moments they are
not together are lamented with the anguish of a longing heart.

Throughout the poem, despite the joys of presence, yearning for
more intimate presence is so strong it seems at times to overshadow the moments together. The lover speaks about seeking and
not finding the beloved. The lover goes out into the night, into the
wilderness, asking everyone where the beloved is.

> I opened to my beloved,
> but my beloved had turned and was gone.
> My soul failed me when he spoke.
> I sought him, but did not find him;
> I called him, but he gave no answer.
> (Song of Songs, 5, 6)

The painful absence of the elusive beloved comes back to haunt
the lover who will not settle for anything less than the felt awareness
of direct presence. Yet, even in the absence of the beloved, a powerful indirect presence can be felt. It seems the heart expands through
desire to accommodate varied forms of presence.

In the poem the lover insists that "love is strong as death, passion fierce as the grave." The lover cries that the fire of love and desire
cannot be quenched, even by floods. The poem ends showing how

absence whets desire, as this great love poem subverts the idea that we feel the power of God only in literal presence.

The Song of Songs was written as a canticle of the love between a man and a woman. It has been taken allegorically as an expression of the intimate relationship between God and the individual human being. It has also been taken as an allegorical expression of the love of God for the people and of Christ for the Church. These symbolic meanings should not lead us to forget its original meaning as a celebration of the sensual delights of love and the lovesickness of the lover for the beloved. But, as mystics have shown, the poem's original meaning is compatible with its use as a description of the longing of the soul for God.

The powerful emotions of the work—the delight of presence, the pain of absence, the yearning and the fulfillment, and above all, the inability to get enough of the beloved—have inspired mystics and poets to use its metaphors for the soul's thirst for the elusive God. Despite the power of its poetic expression, the reader still gets a sense of how hard it is to put into words the desire for God. Beneath the poetic inspiration lies a silent undercurrent that suggests seekers are in over their head when they try to hold on to the elusive God.

The world of intimacy with God hints of an environment not unlike the underwater world. The silent contrast to the noise of daily life, the filtered underwater light that makes everything look different, the support of the water that gives the swimmer a new freedom from gravity—these elements of the deep reveal that there is another reality to which we are usually oblivious. We are not only oblivious to the grace-filled world of intimacy with God; we can feel eerily out of our element in it even though God, like the water of which we are largely composed, is the source of our life. Despite believing God is the source of being, the intimate creator, we are not used to living in full awareness of the presence of that source. And so it is elusive.

Every close relationship, not just our relationship with God, is elusive. No matter how close two human beings are, there is always a zone of mystery that keeps even one who cares deeply for another from fully comprehending the other. That zone of mystery is charged with unanticipated obstacles, vulnerabilities, and underdeveloped skills for accepting mystery. Some of these same challenges face those who aspire to be God's friends, as the Song of Songs shows.

Human intimacy demands attentiveness and trust, and the desire to know God better presents a similar challenge. Just as we become more aware of the other by learning to be increasingly sensitive to a cherished friend, a spouse, or a lover, so also can we become more aware of the presence of mystery when we learn to be attentive to small stirrings of grace. But the mystery always remains. Our spiritual ancestors of the Hebrew Scriptures show us that mystery challenges us all along the road of spiritual growth.

A Message of the Challenges

Each of the challenges our spiritual ancestors confronted tells us something about our own spiritual needs. We often seek God as a means of satisfying our needs—the need for an explanation for suffering, the need for predictability in relationships, the need to feel special, the need to possess the one we love, the need to feel the warmth of God's presence. Enlisting God to serve our perceived needs is a tricky enterprise.

Most of the time we either don't know what we really need or we know what we need only in the very short term. To put it another way, we think of getting what we need in the most direct ways, and we find it hard to imagine God responding to us indirectly.

Job needed to know why he was suffering. Moses needed to know who God would be for him. Jonah needed to feel special. The lover of the Song of Songs needed to know where to find God. All these seekers wanted a God who would meet their needs. But their absorption in their needs sometimes intensified the feeling that God was elusive. This is certainly evident with Jonah.

Jonah wanted a God who made him special, who was exclusively his. The larger God, the God of universal love, eluded him. As a result, he was reluctant to show the mercy that had been shown him. Yet ironically, God gave him what he really needed, which was an opportunity to grow in compassion so that he could know a God bigger than his own ideas of God.

In each of the examples considered, our spiritual ancestors came up against a God who offered opportunities as well as challenges, but spiritual opportunities are not likely to be recognized at the outset when one is looking to satisfy specific needs and desires. Desires are often ego-driven and narrow. When these ancestors learned to lean into the desire planted by God, their more egotistical needs were quieted. Then they could become ready to encounter the hidden God who would enlarge their hearts in silence. If we take time to observe the long view of the spiritual history of Israel, it is possible to see this enlargement as part of a pattern.

In writing of the history of Israel's relationship with God, Richard Elliot Friedman writes of the disappearance of God in Hebrew Scriptures.[2] Friedman says Genesis and Exodus show individuals encountering God directly. After these first direct encounters, there are fewer instances of God's direct communication and fewer miracles. At a second stage of relationship, divine communication comes through selected leaders and prophets. Then, in later books of the Old Testament human beings find themselves having to take on new responsibilities. God is more hidden, sometimes even to leaders and prophets who become models of listening to the elusive God. Friedman does not see this as negative. He says the focus is now on what human beings have to do here in this world. The divine-human relationship takes on more subtle expression.

The elusiveness of God, traced through Hebrew Scriptures, is present also in the Christian Scriptures in which Jesus is proclaimed the Incarnation of God. Those who first followed Jesus, who discovered him to be the great revelation of God's presence, had a lot to learn about the hidden God. When we examine the life and message of Jesus, and the response of his followers to it, we discover that God remains mysterious and elusive even in this Incarnation of God.

3

The Hidden God
in Christian Scripture

Popular Christian culture has at times included stories of encounters with strangers who are hidden manifestations of Christ. One such story is told by the first biographers of Francis of Assisi. As the story goes, early in his conversion Francis encountered a leper as he was riding near Assisi. The sight of the man repulsed him, but his desire to follow Jesus more closely was stronger than his revulsion. He dismounted, rushed to the stranger, and not only gave him money but also kissed his hand. As he returned to his horse and looked around, there was no sign of anyone in any direction. His heart was filled with joy as he realized he had encountered more than a leper. The experience confirmed for him that God is likely to be hidden in the least likely places.

Stories like this carry on the tradition of a hidden God that is central to the Christian Scriptures. In the gospels, the liberating God is shown to dwell among human beings in the person of an obscure Jew. This God is not easily recognized by those looking for signs of majesty and power. It takes an attitude of humility and self-forgetfulness to recognize the presence of God in Jesus. The shepherds at the birth of Jesus, the prostitutes, the disabled, those aware of their sinfulness—these are the ones who are more open to discovering the hidden God in their midst. The poor in spirit can see the invisible God hidden in lowliness and vulnerability.

While the majesty of the transcendent God is hidden, the love of God is made visible in the life and character of the person Jesus. The manifestation of the hidden God in Jesus would seem to remove some of the problems associated with God's hiddenness. In one sense it does and in another sense it doesn't, because not everyone can recognize God in Jesus. It takes a special way of seeing. The embodied presence of God ought to lessen some of the uncertainty about what God is like. If we can see the transcendent power of divine goodness—love, mercy, forgiveness—in a human being, it should be less difficult to know God. Though the gospels show Jesus as exemplifying this transcendent goodness in many ways, they also make it clear that many who knew him were unable to recognize the presence of God in him because he was so ordinary and his message was so revolutionary.

Even John's Gospel, which emphasizes Jesus as a revelation of the divine by speaking of him as the Way, the Truth, and the Life, hints at what is hidden. Jesus may be the way to God, but his way is the road less traveled. Jesus may be the truth, but the truth he reveals is full of paradoxes. Jesus may be the life, but his everlasting life is born from the willingness to die to self.

The followers of Jesus came to be convinced that he was more than the ordinary human being he appeared to be. For Matthew, Mark, and Luke, Jesus is the fulfillment and embodiment of the kingdom of God. For John, Jesus is the Word of God. All the gospels teach that Jesus is the human door to understanding God, but the door opens only by faith. Many who lacked faith were confounded.

We may think that the people of his time had an advantage in being able to see firsthand whether he was a revelation of God. But Jesus was human like the rest of us. For many of the people of his time, Jesus, though spiritually gifted, was no more than a man like other men. They saw him only as an ordinary son of an ordinary carpenter. Even for those with faith, the God within Jesus in some way remained hidden. To appreciate the breadth and depth of God's hiddenness in Jesus, we need to examine the kind of human being Jesus was and the revolutionary nature of his teaching.

God's Hidden Presence in Jesus

Stories about Jesus in the gospels often bring home the point that it takes faith to discover the presence of God in the person of Jesus.

Faith was required whether a person was asking to be cured of disease or was trying to decide if Jesus was the messiah. It took faith to accept this ordinary man as a revelation of God when he lived. It still takes faith.

Those who believe today that God was present uniquely in the person of Jesus and raised to new life have to contend with the same challenges that faced Jesus' early followers. They also need faith to believe that the Spirit of Jesus is present today as the risen Christ in a world where God is still hidden. This faith is tested today, not only because Jesus is no longer physically present but also because the God he reveals is still a mystery.

Even within his historical life, the human Jesus confounded those looking for clear evidence of who he was. To most, he appeared simply as a marginal Jew, an itinerant preacher of Semitic origin who lived a brief, ignominious life. The historical circumstances of his life obscure the God he reveals. People today may have different reasons for failing to see God in Jesus, but the phenomenon of missing the presence of the elusive God is not all that different.

That the elusive God should dwell in a human being bound by the same limitations of gender, ethnicity, and history as any other human being is a paramount example of how hidden God can be. How easy it is to forget that God is present in other limiting situations besides the humanity of Jesus, including in other religious traditions and in other people. Dogmatic insistence that God is present in Jesus and nowhere else can make us miss God's presence in a multitude of forms.

During the time of Jesus, it was not just the person of Jesus that presented a stumbling block; it was his radical religious message that confounded his hearers. The teachings of Jesus, and the methods he used, subvert conventional religious wisdom and replace it with a paradoxical spiritual wisdom. A first step in grasping the wisdom of Jesus' teaching is to be willing to let go of the predictable, domesticated God sanctioned by conventional religion. Jesus' teaching, especially through parables and paradox, subverted his hearers' commonsense understanding of God and how God ought to act. These strategies lead the hearer deeper into the mystery of God.

Parables of the Hidden God

The followers of Jesus once asked him why he taught in parables. This was in some sense a strange question because it was not unusual for teachers of his time to convey their message through parables. Jesus simply followed the usual practice of his day. Nevertheless, Jesus answers their question.

In Matthew's Gospel Jesus tells his followers that he teaches in parables because they have the capacity to know the secrets of heaven; they can grasp the meaning of parables. As for others, Jesus says "seeing they do not perceive, and hearing they do not listen, nor do they understand." He echoes Isaiah, who claims that the hearts of those who do not grasp the parables have grown dull. They have shut their eyes and ears so they cannot understand with their hearts and be healed. He suggests that even religious people may have lost this capacity.

In the same setting, Matthew shows Jesus again quoting the prophet who says that, through parables, what has been hidden will be proclaimed. However, a proclamation through parable does not disclose the hidden message in clear objective terms. In some sense it remains hidden. Unless the individual who hears it can let go of a literal interpretation and can enter into the parable, the meaning of the parable will remain obscure. The hearer must approach the parable with the right attitude.

To appreciate the mystery of God one needs an attitude of openness to the demands of the situation; it is less helpful to fall back on habitual responses or conventional religious practices. The heart of a person needs to be opened so the hidden power of God within the situation can touch that person. At the same time, to penetrate the parables there must be a willingness to enter into the situation presented without overly explaining it. The hidden must be felt, not analyzed.

Among the parables of Jesus, there are many that refer to a hidden God. In each of these, hearers are surprised by a God whom they would not expect to encounter in this situation. Parables such as the parable of the mustard seed, the laborers in the vineyard, or the last judgment, each undermine or subvert a conventional picture of God. They surprise the listener by revealing something unexpected. In each of them, the presence of God makes itself felt as something powerful, and yet for a variety of reasons it could be missed. Some of these parables reveal that the reign of God is hidden from those who rely only on their culture's way of seeing.

Jesus uses the mustard seed to suggest what the kingdom of God is like. The mustard seed is described as the smallest and most insignificant of seeds. Yet it grows to become a large bush that harbors the birds of the field. On one level the ordinary mustard seed is too insignificant to be taken seriously. On another level, because it begins small and grows into something large and wonderful, it is a symbol of faith and the power of God. The power of God is buried within ordinary reality. The smallness and insignificance of ordinary things in nature belie the hidden ability to bring about profound effects.

When influences are hidden or apparently insignificant, we often miss their potential to change things. Forces of nature seem impervious to small influences. But modern science is discovering that is not true. The meteorologist Edward Lorenz discovered that far-reaching effects are possible through the smallest atmospheric changes. While studying weather patterns in computer simulation, he decided to take a shortcut and rounded off a bit of data to the nearest one-thousandth rather than one-millionth decimal. He thought it would make no real difference, but when combined with wind speed, air pressure, and temperature, which were all linked to one another, the difference in the end product was significant. It caused him to wonder whether the flapping of a butterfly's wings in Brazil might cause a tornado in Texas.

Jesus had nothing to say about the butterfly effect, but the examples he often uses in parables suggest that it is not so far-fetched to trust that God's presence, elusive and imperceptible as it may be, can transform persons and even society in a similar way.

Another parable Jesus used to subvert his followers' ideas of God was the parable of the Laborers in the Vineyard. The owner of a vineyard goes out to hire laborers early in the morning and discovers at several points in the day that he still needs workers. Even to the last hour, he keeps returning to hire more workers. When he calls them together to pay them, beginning with the last and ending with the first, he pays them all the same wage.

Predictably, those who worked longest complain. They envy those who had the good fortune to receive as much as they did without working as much. They grumble about the unfairness of the owner. Many of us might agree with them. We expect life to be fair, especially if we hold up our end of the bargain. If we worked harder than others or took our spiritual responsibilities more seriously, we assume we ought to be compensated accordingly. The parable exposes a troubling tendency. It is the ability of comparisons to undermine initial intentions.

The owner responds to those whose comparison leads to discontent. He says that he has paid them what they agreed to, and they have no cause to grumble if he wishes to be generous to those who have less opportunity. There is nothing to suggest the workers were consoled by his explanation. The owner's "unfairness" (or God's) offends them because in their self-righteousness they are prone to comparing. The self-righteous look first at what they "deserve" before considering what others need. They forget how many undeserved blessings they already enjoy.

Jesus unsettles the complacency of his listeners by this parable and leaves them confused about who God is and about their relationship with God. They have to re-think their cherished idea that God favors them because they have earned favor. They have to consider, instead, the mysterious forms of God's goodness toward the outsider, the marginal, and those who do not appear as religious as they.

Finally, one of the most effective parables for showing the hiddenness of God is the parable of the Last Judgment. The last of Matthew's parables about the end of time describes a scene in which the Son of Man gathers the nations at the judgment of the world to announce their fate. Separating them into groups on the right and left as a shepherd would separate the sheep and goats, he says to those on the right that they will inherit the kingdom. He tells them they are blessed because when he was hungry they fed him, when he was thirsty they gave him drink, when he was naked they clothed him. These generous ones are astounded and ask when they extended these mercies to him. They were not aware it was he. The judge answers that when they did it for the least ones, they did it for him.

When he turns to those on the left, he tells them they will not enter God's kingdom because when he was hungry they did not feed him, when he was thirsty they gave him no drink, when he was naked they did not clothe him. Ironically, those who failed to extend mercy give the same response. They ask when it was that they saw him hungry, thirsty, naked, a stranger, sick, or in prison. The judge answers that when they failed to have compassion on those in need, they failed to have compassion for him.

This classic parable of the hidden God captures a theme that runs through the Christian Scriptures. Service to one's brothers and sisters is service to God. Love of one's sisters and brothers is love of God. Because God's presence is always hidden, especially among those who are easily overlooked, Jesus reminds his listeners they need to perceive what is not visible through ordinary sight. Through the parables Jesus offers a view of God that is in some ways more tangible and, at the same time, less graspable.

One of the striking aspects of this approach is an inclusiveness and breadth of perception that is larger than that of conventional religion. Conventional religion offers a set of beliefs and practices that follows a certain religious logic, such as "suffering is a punishment from God" or "do good so you will be rewarded." It provides a framework to understand how things work religiously and what to expect. It suggests how to think of God and what to expect if we engage in certain behavior.

Conventional religion provides us with a familiar road to God. But we are just as likely to encounter God on side roads or in unfamiliar circumstances. The message of Jesus often undermines conventional religious wisdom. His vision subverts the tried and true and opens the way to discover a larger, more inclusive God through paradox.

Paradox as a Sign of Hiddenness

Jesus' teachings, like the teachings of Zen masters, cannot be reduced to a rational philosophy. His message can't be explained as if it involves a set of rules that just need to be memorized and unpacked. Some people have tried to treat it this way. They have tried to present him as a great ethical teacher or as a motivational speaker. When they do this, they look at one side of his message and neglect the aspects of his preaching that point to a God of mystery. By pointing to a hidden God, Jesus coaxes his followers to move beyond their comfort zone to *terra incognita*, the unknown land that beckons spiritual explorers.

Just as it is much more comfortable to speak of Jesus only as an advocate of loving one's neighbor than to speak of his challenge to love our enemies, it is much more comfortable to think of him as a confirmation of our customary reasoning about God than as a revelation of a God who transcends our understanding. But that is what Jesus is.

The God who is hidden in Jesus turns our conventional values and behavior upside down. Jesus presents a new perspective that destabilizes his followers' relationship to their world through a series of paradoxes. He tells them that unless they lose themselves they will not find themselves, that he came not to bring peace but a sword, that the last shall be first and the first last. And, as Paul put the central paradox, Jesus lived a life that showed that the cross, which is foolishness to the world, is God's wisdom. His followers do not grasp what he is about unless they accept these paradoxes as leading to deeper truths that are not accessible through ordinary language or thought processes.

Whatever else a paradox connotes, it signals an undermining of expectations. The word *paradox* derives from the roots *para* (beyond, or sometimes against) and *doxa* (opinion or belief). A paradox goes against what we ordinarily believe or expect, what makes sense to us. What makes it a paradox and not just nonsense is that it also points to a deeper or more comprehensive truth.

Paradox is an apparently self-contradictory statement that is, nevertheless, true, even though it undermines what we usually think of as truth. We often fail to realize how much "common sense" has colored our ideas of God. We are in the habit of acting as if we can fit God into our ordinary, limited ways of thinking. Jesus devoted himself to trying to get his followers to realize that this was not the case. They would have to let go of the conventional religious thinking they were used to and start living within another value system where paradox flourishes.

The values Jesus offered are summarized in the Sermon on the Mount, in which his revolutionary teaching reaches a climax. The Sermon on the Mount in Matthew's Gospel, a distillation of Jesus' message, begins with the beatitudes. Each of the eight beatitudes reverses our expectations about what brings happiness, beginning with "Blessed are the poor in spirit; the kingdom of heaven is theirs." Some are less paradoxical than others, but there is no escaping the reversal of expectation in statements like "blessed are they who mourn," "blessed are the meek," and "blessed are those who are persecuted." God bestows blessings in the least likely situations.

The Sermon on the Mount includes some practical advice about praying and obeying the law, but it also weaves in impractical advice like loving one's enemies and not worrying about where our next meal is coming from. This impractical advice is part of the strategy the sermon uses to destabilize a too-familiar religious atmosphere. It hints of the strange and hidden God who graces people in the oddest ways. The sermon does not reassure those who are looking for religion only to comfort them.

Jesus consoled those in need of comfort, but he seems to have found it just as important to unsettle those who were too comfortable. He challenged more than their view of God, however. His teaching went to the heart of their understanding of the self that encounters the hidden God.

The Hidden God and the Hidden Self

Jesus said some things about God that appeared quite direct. He taught his followers to address God in prayer as "Our Father," whom he also referred to more intimately as "Abba." He spoke of himself, in John's Gospel, as the way to God, and he spoke of God abiding in him and himself abiding in God. And yet, he also suggests he knows God indirectly. He speaks of not knowing when the end time will come. He asks God that he not to have to suffer *unless* it is God's will. He speaks of feeling abandoned on the cross.

In short, in Jesus we find elements of a great intimacy with God and, at the same time, elements of mystery and unknowing. It is to the credit of those who remembered his words and actions that they preserved the paradox. If Jesus is to be a model of what it means to be fully human, he has to embody the limits of the human situation as well as its possibilities. At the center of his humanity, encompassing its depths and heights, his words and actions came forth from a hidden self.

The hidden self of Jesus was the core of his being where he was united with God in prayer, in hope, and in compassion. We can never know how he encountered the hidden God in the depths of his hidden self. We can't know the self of another person directly any more than we can know our own selves directly. While the culture in which Jesus lived did not think in terms of *self*, hidden or otherwise, we can glean from Jesus' teachings some important lessons about the dangers of paying too much attention to the things we associate with self.

Jesus tried to guide his followers away from preoccupation with self when he spoke of losing the self and finding the self. His own self is so profoundly hidden in the mystery of a hidden God that we have no idea when or how he came to this understanding. But we know it is important enough that he impressed it on those who followed him.

Whenever Jesus' followers start to fall back into their old habits of thinking, he cautions them. He says if they want to save their selves, they must lose them for a greater good. They should not seek the first places. They should not seek power or hold on to it. These activities are the work of the narrow ego. But his hearers often miss his point and continue to operate out of the same ego concerns.

Peter protests that he will not let Jesus suffer because it is not fitting for the Messiah. Others quarrel about who will be first in the kingdom because they want to maintain a privileged position. The common criteria for success and failure still dominate their thinking and cloud their ability to see the wisdom in the paradox of dying to self in order to live. It takes time for them to grow in understanding so that they can grasp the identity of Jesus and his hidden relationship with God. Only then will they be freed from their servitude to the small self which is the ego.

If Jesus tried to make people aware of ego in a culture that didn't have a clear concept of ego, how much more should we be aware of it in a culture that elevates ego to the level of an icon. Everything in the culture that surrounds us demands we save the self—by consuming, by competing, by controlling. But the self we are urged to save is the narrow ego that must protect itself at any cost. This ego cannot be saved. It will always remain subject to threat, so it will constantly need to be defended.

The hidden self, which does not need to be defended, is the self that abides in the hidden God. This is the self to which Paul refers when he says "it is no longer I who live, but it is Christ who lives in me." The "I" that no longer lives is the singular ego that tries to make its way through life independently of God. The self hidden in God becomes more and more the center of life and activity as it was for Jesus himself.

In the centuries after Jesus died, his followers reflected on his identity and his intimate relationship with God. They believed that in his existence and in the way he lived, he made the hidden God transparent. Paradox still proved useful in the sense that now it allowed his followers to speak of him as both human and divine. But because paradoxes perplex those who want clarity, theologians began to work to make the meaning of Jesus more accessible.

Theologians pondered, beyond the pages of Scripture and the holy rites of their worship, how to speak of a God who is one and yet trinity, and who is hidden yet present uniquely in the person of Jesus of Nazareth. Those who tried to shed light on the presence of God in Jesus, ultimately found themselves drawn back into mystery. They had to admit, sooner or later, that God remains elusive. The next chapter follows their exploration from its beginning to the present.

4

God of the Theologians

As we saw in the Christian Scriptures, even if one considers God to be incarnate in Jesus, the mystery of a hidden God remains. Theology can help in approaching that mystery. For the beginning of Christian theology, we need to turn to Saint Paul. Theological insights permeate all his writings, but we get the first hint of his theology in his preaching as Luke records it in the Acts of the Apostles.

Luke recounts a visit of Paul to Athens, where he preached about Jesus and the God of Jesus. To make his preaching understandable in this culture, Paul looks for a point of contact. He notes that there was an altar inscribed with a dedication to the unknown god. Paul tells the Athenians that the god they described as unknown is the God who created the world, the same God who raised Jesus from the dead. And so, there in Athens, Christian theology is born.

In order to get the Athenians to consider the message of Jesus, Paul had to make a connection between their way of thinking and Christian faith. This involved building on the Greek respect for reason. Paul wasn't really interested in getting into a philosophical debate. He knew that human reasoning can take you only so far, that God's wisdom is greater than any philosophy. But he also understood that faith had to be communicated to other believers and to those who were potential believers. Theology helps to do this.

Theology is a reflection on, an explication of, faith within a religious tradition. In Christianity, faith has relied heavily on reasoning and on philosophical principles. This reliance derives in part from the influence of Greek philosophers who believed that, as "rational animals," human beings seek beliefs that make sense. Or, at least they seek beliefs that are not unreasonable. Within several centuries after Jesus died, educated Christians, influenced by a Greek mentality, began to use philosophical concepts to explain their beliefs. Philosophy provided a framework for theologians to make Christianity intelligible by giving them a language that would be understood by those who lived in the world where they taught.

At first, Christian thinkers like Tertullian were wary of getting caught up in philosophical discourse. Tertullian asked, "What indeed has Athens to do with Jerusalem?" What does the academy of philosophical discourse have to do with the community of worship? The last thing he wanted to see was Christianity muddled up with Stoic and Platonic concepts. He tried to avoid philosophical debates, first because he was a practical Roman and somewhat less philosophical than those of Greek heritage. More important, Tertullian did not want to see Christianity take on too much of the thought and values of the culture. But in time Christianity's need for philosophical thinking seemed more pressing.

The early Christians were faced with charges that they were enemies of the Roman Empire and therefore should be persecuted. In order to defend themselves from wild rumors, they had to rely on reasoning that made sense to the world in which they lived. When Christianity became acceptable and Christians no longer had to respond to these charges, they continued to use reason and philosophy in order to make their faith understood and intellectually respectable for an increasingly educated populace.

It wasn't long before Greek philosophy, considered to be the zenith of intellectual life, became an instrument for teaching the meaning of Jesus Christ and the Christian God. Some proponents of Greek philosophy went so far as to present Christ as the true philosopher. They saw him embodying a vision of rationality, as Jaroslav Pelikan puts it, by providing "the divine clue to the structure of reality."[1]

In the culture where Christianity was spreading, theologians used philosophy in various ways to reflect on and articulate their God to others. Origen, who lived in the late second and early third centuries, used philosophical concepts creatively to help people think about God. Instead of simply accepting the nature of God as unchangeable and above human emotion, Origen stretched the customary way of thinking and presented God as passionate and merciful. He saw God as always at work, guiding human beings through the use of their freedom, leading the universe slowly toward a harmonious unity. But he understood God's guidance of history to be hidden.

Origen also saw the meaning of Scripture as hidden. He highlighted the importance of looking beyond the words of Scripture to its symbolic meaning, a meaning that becomes known only after one lives reflectively in its presence. Living reflectively in the presence of mystery also describes the attitude of a group of theologians from the eastern part of the Roman Empire who emphasized the mystery of God.

Negative Theology

There was a tradition among Eastern theologians (those who flourished in Greek-influenced rather than Roman-influenced countries) that promoted an austere attitude toward speaking about God.[2] Many theologians believed no words were adequate to speak of God. Gregory of Nyssa wrote in the fourth century that when it comes to God, seeing consists in "not seeing, because that which is sought transcends all knowledge, being separated on all sides by incomprehensibility." The knowledge of God is a dark knowledge. Unless a person experiences it, such knowledge cannot be imagined. Even when experienced, words are inadequate to convey it.

The approach that emphasizes the incomprehensibility of God is sometimes referred to as negative theology or apophatic theology. If theology refers to speech about God, then apophatic theology refers to "that speech about God which is the failure of speech."[3] Denys Turner writes that negative or apophatic theology rests on the idea that absence, otherness, and difference are better reference points for God than more positive images, which can seduce us into thinking we know something specific about God.[4]

Kataphatic theology, in contrast to apophatic theology, uses diverse forms of language to describe God. God as beauty, wisdom, father, mother, king, rock, and many more images provide an explosion of possibilities for imagining God. This array of images and metaphors seems to say a great deal; yet even a full collection of metaphors doesn't say enough. Language strains under the burden of the meaning of the divine. Furthermore, because we cannot absorb such a surplus of meaning, we tend to cling to one image and to treat it as sufficient.

No single image, or collection of images, can capture the fullness of what we mean when we say "God." Complete silence about God is also inadequate. So, both apophatic and kataphatic approaches are needed in order to correct one another and to convey the fullness of God's being, which remains beyond comprehension.

While the kataphatic approach is familiar and comfortable to most people, apophatic theology seems to be growing more influential in our age. It is attractive in particular to those for whom the familiar God has "disappeared" and who want to find a way to think of God that fits with their experience. The appeal of apophatic theology to contemporary thinkers may also be influenced by a new awareness of the cultural conditioning of language and thought, and therefore the problem of placing too much trust in them. Because negative theology has some contemporary appeal, however, we should not assume that it is a modern invention. Its roots reach deep into the Christian tradition.

One of the earliest champions of "negative theology" was Dionysius the Areopagite or Pseudo-Dionysius, as he was more commonly known.[5] Pseudo-Dionysius was originally thought to be a first-century convert of Saint Paul, but contemporary scholars believe he wrote from Syria, possibly as late as the sixth century. Dionysius says we cannot say what God is, but only what God is not. He asserted that God must be experienced in silence because the Mystery of the Godhead "exceeds all Mind and Being."

Maximus the Confessor wrote a commentary on Pseudo-Dionysius in the seventh century. Inspired by his theology, Maximus wrote that the inaccessible God is beyond affirmation *and* negation. One can only approach God in silence and awareness of one's own ignorance. As Maximus puts it, "For the ignorance about God on the part of those who are wise in divine things is not a lack of learning, but a knowledge that knows by silence that God is unknown." For

Maximus, then, this ignorance or unknowing is not a lazy refusal to ponder God but the culmination of a quest that ends in awe.

The comment of Maximus about wisdom in divine things reveals a profound but inarticulate knowledge of God. Those who come to know God through reverent silence have wrestled with God and matured in faith. They have come to an acceptance of the mystery of God at the end of a process of struggling to understand the God beyond mere concepts. They do not use the incomprehensibility of God as an excuse for not embarking on the journey to wisdom.

Eastern theologians were thoroughly imbued with a sense of God's incomprehensibility, but they also believed, paradoxically, that human beings are destined for deification, or transformation into the likeness of God. Though human beings cannot comprehend God through reasoning, they can become God-like. This statement is not as much of a contradiction as it might sound.

As Maximus put it, "No creature is capable of deification by its own nature, since it is not capable of grasping God. This can happen only with the grace of God." The inability of human beings to know God intellectually does not get in the way of God's ability to transform us spiritually. Deification has to do with transformation, not information.

Though God is ultimately beyond our comprehension, it is possible to speak of knowledge of God in a way that is analogous to knowledge of self. The way we know ourselves involves intuitive understanding and subtle insights that cannot be reduced to a set of data. Personal knowledge of our inner history, of our sincerity or insincerity, of our psychological and spiritual conflicts and the way we resolve them, of the weight of our motivations—such knowledge depends on intuition and cannot be fully articulated. We know God through intuition as well, but that intuition is much more difficult to express.

Whenever we try to understand the interplay between God's grace, which stirs us unbidden, and our efforts to find God, the relationship is hidden in darkness. Whenever we try to give voice to holy hunger for the divine, we cannot be sure exactly what it is we are seeking and what God is calling us to. As we come to realize the difficulty of speaking of a relationship with God, we are left with a greater awareness of what we do not know of ourselves and of God. The lack of full and clear knowledge is compatible with what theologians describe as the human destiny for deification. Roman-influenced theologians were not quite so intrigued by the mysterious deification of human beings or by the limits of language about God. They spoke more positively of God (and sometimes more negatively of human beings), using concepts and images that were familiar to their listeners. Yet, in the end, they were not reluctant to admit the limits of their knowledge. Beginning with the Middle Ages, these theologians provide us with some outstanding examples of the blending of positive and negative theology.

Developments in the Theology of a Hidden God

Among Latin theologians, the hiddenness and ineffability of God was not as strong a theme as it was among Greek theologians. Latin theologians seemed more taken up with ideas of order and practicality when discussing God. But the hiddenness of God was not ignored. Instead, it found expression different from that of the darker tradition of the mysterious God, spoken of by theologians like Gregory of Nyssa or Maximus.

Saint Augustine of Hippo, who was born in the fourth century, was strongly influenced by Plato. Augustine built on Plato's philosophy by developing a theology that turned inward and upward as it stretched toward infinite mystery. While Augustine felt that the senses are useful as stepping-stones, he believed a person needed to transcend the senses in order to ascend toward spiritual knowledge.

In his *Confessions*, Augustine searches his soul for traces of God's presence because he already believes God is "deeply hidden yet most intimately present."[6] Like Plato, he is convinced that one must rise above the material world, which can obscure the presence of God. The more the mind moves away from the changing world toward the realm of unchanging, eternal ideas, the more it approaches the mystery of God.

But Augustine does not say that the limited human mind can grasp the infinite God on its own by accessing a hidden human understanding; he says that to know God one needs the light of God that teaches truth. The light of God is a grace that brings knowledge human beings are incapable of attaining on their own. Just as important, one needs to surrender to the hidden mystery of God instead of trying to figure it out.

Augustine is completely convinced of God's presence always and everywhere, but he believes that human beings are sometimes unable to grasp God's presence. The inability to appreciate God's presence comes not only from the hiddenness of God but can also come from sin. Sin clouds the mind so it is more difficult for the light of grace to penetrate it.

When sin clouds the mind, it leads one to believe that God is not just hidden, but distant. The distance between God and the sinner comes in large part from the sinner hiding from God, which then makes it difficult to perceive God's presence. Augustine felt keenly the results of estrangement because of sin. Yet he knew that even aside from sin, the mystery of God remains.

Augustine's theology continued to have great influence over the centuries. But in the thirteenth century, as the physical world assumed a greater importance than Augustine's theology allowed, a new approach began to take hold. While some, like Bonaventure, continued to be influenced by Plato's philosophical thought, Thomas Aquinas found Aristotle's approach better suited for his purposes because it took the physical world more seriously. Aquinas felt that human knowledge depends on what can be observed in the world through the senses. The senses, illuminated by reason, provide a starting point for understanding the world, an understanding that can lead a person to God.

Sense knowledge can lead to God by providing the conditions to reflect on God. In examining the conditions found in nature, reason concludes certain things about God—that God is the source and origin of causality, motion, contingency, design, and perfection. While it is possible to defend the existence of God through these "proofs,"

Aquinas held that the reasoning behind them cannot reveal what God is like. For that, revelation and grace are needed.

When it comes to speaking about God, reason and revelation complement each other. Reason allows a person to speak credibly of the existence of God. It also makes it possible to develop a theology. Revelation, in contrast, allows a person to root speech about God in a source deeper than reason. Revelation is a divine disclosure and not the result of deduction. Reason depends on human effort; revelation depends on God's gift.

Yet Aquinas is careful to acknowledge the limits of knowledge of God. He says, "We cannot know what God is, but only what he is not."[7] Though Aquinas clearly recognized the inability of human beings to comprehend God, he may have felt the impact of that realization only intellectually at first. It took a religious experience to impress on him how powerless human thought is to capture the meaning of God. After this experience, he saw his theological work as so much straw. He stopped doing theology before he completed his great *Summa*.

Several centuries after Aquinas, in the sixteenth century, Martin Luther reacted more negatively to the efforts of theology to make statements about God. Theology had become academic. It seemed to make God remote and inaccessible. Luther believed that the only way a Christian could know God was through faith in Christ and the Bible. It was only Scripture, and ultimately only faith, that would keep the believer from despairing over the elusive God.

Luther lived at the threshold of the modern world, but he was still in the world of Christendom where believers relied on certain ideas, practices, and symbols as part of their faith life. He saw these accessories of faith as part of a religious world dominated by monastic prayer, the papacy, the priesthood, and religious life, as well as in practices like obtaining indulgences. All of these, it seemed to him, were part of a theology that got in the way of direct access to God.

Luther emphasized a radical faith in God that called for the personal commitment of the individual. The individual became the focus, not just in Luther's time but as his influence continued. The church he founded moved into a world where the individual came more and more to be the focus in society. But the individual can often feel alone, without adequate support for the kind of faith Luther encouraged. A personal commitment to faith in a God who remains hidden is not easy to sustain. Without the support of others, individuals longing for God may lose heart.

When we turn to the twentieth century, the practical problem of individualism is compounded by cultural conditions that make the hidden presence of God more difficult to perceive. Whether the challenge to faith comes from science, philosophy, or crises in society, the work of theologians demands a new sensitivity to God. Of the many theologians who have tried to deal creatively with the "disappearing" God, two stand out as particularly influential.

Paul Tillich, a German Lutheran theologian who emigrated to the United States, saw theology as a dialogue between faith and the world in which it is lived out. The basic question that provokes the dialogue for him is the question of human finitude.[8] Human beings know that they are finite, that they will die, but they long for the Infinite from which they are estranged. When they look for the infinite God, seekers in today's world do not find the God they've been led to expect.

In responding to this dilemma, Tillich does not rely on traditional ways of speaking of God, but instead reconsiders the way we speak of God. To speak or think of God as a supreme being puts God in the category of one among other beings. It limits God. For Tillich, God is not *a* Being but Being-Itself, the Ground of Being, or the goal of Ultimate Concern. The objective of spiritual life is not to rediscover a being that has disappeared but to discover the hidden God beyond God.

Karl Rahner offers another perspective on the hidden God. Rahner also begins with the experience of the human subject.[9] He approaches human beings as transcendent, or open to God and others. Because they are transcendent, human beings are capable of knowing in subtle ways. Human beings come to experience God not as they might experience *things* in their world, but pre-consciously as they would experience their sense of self and personal continuity. This opens up a way of knowing God that is more like horizon or background than foreground. It is an intuitive awareness that underlies other kinds of knowing. This way of knowing disposes persons toward the "incomprehensible and ineffable Mystery" that is God.

As we can see from this wide-ranging glance over Western theology since the time of Augustine, theologians have consistently remained aware of the need to remind their listeners that God is mystery. The theologies of our present age need to find their own ways to do the same.

Theology in an Age of Longing

The theologians considered so far all attempted to make Christian faith intelligible. That inevitably meant saying something about God. But the best of them all knew that their theology could not be the last word. There is no last word; ultimately God is mystery. Theologians today must remember this, even though they need to do all they can to make faith intelligible in a changing world.

When theologians seek to make faith comprehensible in their own time, they help to preserve Christian tradition as it adapts to new situations. They may use traditional philosophical frameworks to help believers make connections between faith and experience. Or like theologians today, they may use modern philosophies like process philosophy and existentialism. Whatever tools are used, theology ought to serve the spiritual life of people.

If theologians are to serve those who desire to know God, their theology needs to be integrated with spirituality. Theology represents the mind of faith as it clarifies the content of a religious tradition. Spirituality represents the heart of faith in its living expressions. When theology and spirituality are integrated, the heart and the mind of the God-seeker are nourished, and action is as important as faith.

The early Greek theologians demonstrated this kind of integration. Their theology was guided by a concern for the spiritual life and not just by a concern to make God intelligible. They did not lose sight of pastoral concerns for the faith and prayer life of people who encountered the living God through the ebb and flow of light and darkness. We have something to learn from them in an age in which

God is not as evident as before. They tell us that just because we cannot speak easily of what God is, that does not mean we must wander without any direction in an age of skepticism.

Theology in the twenty-first century faces a huge challenge. It needs to speak intelligibly of God and yet always be willing to critique its own language. It needs to offer encouragement to those who do not find God as evident as before and yet avoid suggesting easy ways of finding God. Theology needs to teach us to be aware of the way we have been conditioned to think about God and attentive to the possibilities of opening ourselves to the actions demanded by the hidden presence of God today.

The theology that encourages us to be attentive to a God we have missed will be marked by an attitude that is both prophetic and contemplative. Prophetically, it will direct us to recognize and deal with whatever in our faith threatens to become idolatrous. Contemplatively, it will keep us from becoming immersed in the superficial aspects of faith to the neglect of its deeper truths.

When theology is prophetic, it tries to avoid idolatrous attitudes that can accompany certain ideas of God. It is easy to be blind to our own biases and to fail to notice that we have made an idol of a particular notion of God. When we prefer a God who has attributes of a dominant class (white, European, male, etc.), or who favors those who work hard and become successful, or who establishes religious rules to separate the worthy and the unworthy, we risk creating an idol. Theology that accepts the challenge to be prophetic remains aware of its tendency to reflect the biases of those who write it. When theology defends a privileged position, it is all too easy to forget the hidden God.

Theology ought to always be ready to surrender its prejudices, to clear a path for the hidden God. Because of its longing to know the true God, the God who cannot be defined by anyone with vested interests, theology needs to be impelled by a desire to avoid self-deception. This theology and the spirituality it fosters teach us to exercise a critical, loving judgment on ideas and actions, so that we can discover God's truth.

When theology is contemplative, it is open to the God who is hidden everywhere. The starting point of such a theology is an attitude of reverence and awe before God rather than concern to argue or make a point. Theology activated by a contemplative attitude puts prayer and responsive listening before the desire to defend a position. Such a theology comes from a heart that longs for God's truth first.

To ground theology in a contemplative attitude is to strive first to be present to the Presence. It is to allow oneself to be found by God before expounding on God. For all the importance of knowing one's tradition and knowing the contemporary world, there is little likelihood that theology can minister to the God-seeker without being rooted in the most basic human condition.

A contemplative attitude complements a prophetic attitude. The prophet senses when it is time to critique ideas and actions, and the contemplative senses when it is time to accept what is. A contemplative approach puts the intellectual dimension in second place to the beauty and mystery of the God who waits to be received, not seized.

We need women and men of keen theological intellect, like the classic spiritual theologians, who can guide us in the direction of integration. We need theologians with excellent powers of analysis to expose the subtle forms of idolatry that can creep into our vision of God. But we also need women and men of imagination and humility who can help us articulate, within our limits, the God who makes the heart restless. We need men and women with large hearts who will encourage us not to settle for too easy answers.

One woman who stands out as an example of this viewpoint is the French mystic Simone Weil. While not a theologian or even a baptized Christian, she wrote as a prophet and contemplative convinced that any human being can penetrate to the kingdom of truth if only they long for it and concentrate all their attention on its attainment.[10] For Weil, concentrating attention means not only working at it but also waiting contemplatively.

Weil was convinced that the desire for truth, beauty, and goodness has an effectiveness in the spiritual realm it may have nowhere else. She believed that desire and longing, when attended to with heartfelt attention, lead steadily to God, even though God remains hidden. For someone like Weil, every age is an age of longing.

While theologians can cultivate prophetic and contemplative attitudes, they are not always in positions that allow them to strengthen these attitudes. Since theologians often serve the church or the academy, they can be under pressure to defend the views of these institutions. It is mystics like Weil who challenge theologians to be courageous in insisting on the hiddenness of God.

Christianity's own mystics are in a good position to complement the work of theologians in articulating the mystery of God. The next chapter will reflect on the insights of this last group of spiritual ancestors who help us deal with the hidden God.

5

God of the Mystics

While theologians depend on concepts and ideas to put across an understanding of God, mystics soar above the mind's usual path. Their flight is characterized more by lively imagery than by philosophical ideas. The extravagant imagery that mystics use, born of the intensity of their absorption in God, stretches language about God.

The language of mystics often blurs the distinction between human beings and God, and calls attention to their intense desire for the presence of God. Hadewijch of Brabant describes union with God as the absorption of herself into God and God into her.

> I saw him completely come to naught and so fade and all at once dissolve that I could no longer recognize or perceive him outside me, and I could no longer distinguish him within me. Then it was to me as if we were one without difference.[1]

Hadewijch speaks of this vision of union with God as a culmination of her longing for God, a longing that can neither be expressed in language nor understood by those who have never desired it or perceived it as something to work for. Because the longing cannot be expressed in language, and certainly not in ordinary language, mystics are likely to use extravagant language filled with sensual images. The most sensual language and images often arise out of extraordinary visions that suggest a direct experience of God. But direct experience and visions are not required for mystical consciousness.

Mysticism is often spoken of as a direct experience of God. It is a matter of debate whether it is possible for finite human beings to "experience" the infinite God. It would seem that we can only speak of beings as experiencing other limited beings. To speak of experiencing God is not to refer to the experience of a specific object. Mysticism is better understood as a felt awareness of connection. As Bernard McGinn puts it, "Mysticism is characterized by a sense of an immediate relation to God and the transformation this effects."[2] The awareness of relationship with God does not depend on visions or extraordinary religious experiences.

Mystics have sometimes given accounts of particular experiences, like visions, that reveal God to them. But these visions are not essential to mysticism, and gifted guides caution about paying much attention to them. Sometimes a special experience like a vision may open a door to knowledge of God, but what is more reliable than visions is an abiding awareness of God and a desire for God. The abiding awareness of relationship or connection disposes a person to a life of greater union with God.

The desire for union with God has been seen by some spiritual writers as the driving force of a spiritual journey with God. Classically, the journey leading to union with God has been interpreted as consisting of stages of deepening absorption in God. Saint Bonaventure, writing in the Middle Ages when mysticism reached a peak, provides a thorough description of this spiritual process as it was understood then.

The Triple Way

Saint Bonaventure offers a description of stages in the spiritual life as a kind of map of the journey of the soul to God. In *The Triple Way* Bonaventure describes and explains the maturing of spiritual life as a person's transformation into the image of Christ through three phases of developing intimacy with God.[3] This thirteenth-century Franciscan sees Saint Francis of Assisi as a prime example of the way the transformation occurs.

Bonaventure outlines the progress of spiritual life as an ascent through purgation and illumination to union with God. The first stage is purgation, which begins when individuals recognize their sinfulness and turn away from what keeps them from becoming like Christ. It represents a purification of sinful and selfish behavior, instincts, habits, and attitudes. In this early stage of transformation into the likeness of Christ, a person becomes increasingly aware of attachment to selfish desires and things that are not God. The person focuses on the discipline of getting rid of old bad habits and acquiring new beneficial attitudes. Prayer becomes more regular, vices are repudiated, and conscious effort is made to do good. This stage takes effort. Though it can be very hard, it often involves a sense of satisfaction that one is on the right path.

The second stage in the ascent to God is called illumination, and it begins when an individual sees the light of true Godly living, especially as it is expressed in the person of Jesus. This phase refers to a stage of spiritual life in which the person considers not only God's forgiveness of sin but also the gifts of nature, divine assistance, and Jesus Christ himself. Christ is teacher and model of what human beings are to become: the likeness of God. Jesus is the Light and the Way. To study his life and his words, to strive to mirror his virtues, is to enter more fully into Christian life. Discipline is sweeter and less labored than it is in the purgative stage. Though effort is needed in the stage of illumination, a clearer vision makes effort less arduous. The hardship involved in being a disciple seems little compared to gratitude for God's gifts.

The third and ultimate stage of spiritual growth comes in union with God. Here awareness of the presence of God inflames desire. A degree of union is experienced, and, at the same time, a greater degree is desired. Paradoxically, as the wisdom that accompanies deepening union grows, the ordinary way of knowing darkens. At this stage, says Bonaventure, the Beloved is above anything "perceptible, imaginable or conceivable." The Beloved has no "shape, figure, quantity, limitation, or mutability." The Beloved is beyond "demonstration, definition, opinion, estimation, or investigation." Despite the blockage of the ordinary paths of knowledge, Bonaventure repeatedly says that the Beloved is "all delight."

In this third stage of the journey to God, the seeker is less active. The striving of purgation and illumination ceases, and so does the effort to acquire virtue. The person who actively sought God now becomes passive. The individual begins to realize it is God who has been doing the seeking, and the seeker now waits to be found.

Bonaventure finds this pattern to be characteristic of those who are serious about the God quest. He observes people who start out as sinners and begin a process of conversion. He watches them as they find a guide or model to direct them toward their goal and keep them on track. He notes that when they pursue their goal faithfully, they intensify desire for union with God and participate in that union even though they know it is incomplete. Bonaventure generalizes that this pattern will hold true for others.

Bonaventure was too wise a spiritual guide to think that a person would move mechanically through these stages. His discernment of the spirit allowed him to see elements of the stages intermingled. But because the culture in which he wrote was permeated more by the language of faith than ours is, we hear in his words clear distinctions and a greater measure of certainty than is likely when we read the works of spiritual development in our own culture.

Bonaventure's culture perceived a divinely ordered world where everything had its place and its logic. New contexts or developments didn't alter anything. Once a person was on the right track from purgation through illumination to union, external circumstances didn't matter. We who live in a rapidly changing world often find ourselves in new situations that challenge this view. We are too aware of the constancy of change to believe that we can arrive at the experience of union once and for all. We are too aware of the life-altering effects of cultural, social, and personal change to expect an analysis of spiritual growth to yield a pattern that fits all persons. Living in the context of constant change, we find it especially hard to maintain confidence that the hidden God is present in everything that is fragmentary and in flux.

Yet there is truth in Bonaventure's vision, even though its orderliness sounds too predictable and appears more convincing in its medieval context than in today's context. People do experience periods of purgation and illumination similar to what he describes. They do relate experiences of oneness and desire. However, the orderly style of a medieval presentation does not capture the flavor of contemporary experience. So we need to interpret them within our own framework.

Purgation, illumination, and union can be involved simultaneously at every stage of the religious journey. They may or may not occur in a particular order. They are present in different ways depending on the circumstances at a given time in the journey to God. Even when one experiences a degree of union, the desire for greater union brings about a new purgation or purification.

Purification appears in the midst of desire for union when a person has to face a God who has become more hidden. This is evident in Bonaventure's description of the Beloved as beyond perception, imagination, concepts, definition, or investigation. According to his suggestion, it is in the midst of union with God that God is most hidden. So while the triple way can help our understanding of the spiritual life, at its culmination in union with God it breaks the boundaries of thought and language. Some mystical writers after Bonaventure took this further and offered provocative new images of the hidden God.

Clouds, Hidden Unity, and Darkness: Lessons from the Mystics

Writers on mystical union in the spiritual life give us further insights into the way serious God-seekers might deal with the elusiveness of God. *The Cloud of Unknowing*, the work of an anonymous English monk of the fourteenth century, is one example of such counsel.[4] The stated purpose of the work was to provide guidance for a young man who was considering the contemplative life. The author tries to help the young man decide by describing what it takes to be a contemplative. In the process he also describes the attitudes necessary to dispose oneself to union with a hidden God.

The author cautions that no one should bother reading the book who is not serious about being a follower of Christ and who is not already experienced in this pursuit. The way he proposes is for those who are drawn by "an inward stirring toward the secret spirit of God whose judgments are hidden." This hidden God eludes ordinary religious ways.

Persons drawn by God's spirit, he says, should not cling to tangible expressions of God, no matter how holy or proper they may seem. Even lofty thoughts of saints, Jesus, and God are to be ignored. "For even though it is good to think about the kindness of God, and to love Him and to praise Him for it, nevertheless it is far better to think about His naked being and to praise Him and love Him for Himself." Those who truly desire God should be willing and humble enough not to depend on mind or imagination. They should be ready to enter the cloud of unknowing.

The author of *The Cloud of Unknowing* is not talking about a cloud of obscurity that temporarily prevents a person from understanding. We anticipate such a cloud will disappear if we try hard enough to penetrate it. He is speaking of a cloud that will not disappear. The cloud of unknowing is a spiritual cloud, a spiritual mystery. The reader is not to try to remove this mystery or to seek an image of God that is more esoteric. She or he has only to lift the heart in love. If this seems more than they can manage, it is sufficient to offer God the "naked intent of the will." The naked intent of the will is the *desire* to love God, not for any spiritual gain but simply because of the goodness of God.

What is essential for mystics like the author of *The Cloud* is that the seeker desires God as God is, not as God might be thought of or imagined. Thus, the path with God must be marked by forgetfulness of all that is not the cloud.

A similar theme is struck by the German mystic Meister Eckhart. Eckhart holds that we are so united to God already that the only thing that separates us is the desire to be separate, to be an ego. It is because of the perception that we are separate, and the desire to be separate, that we perceive God as hidden and elusive.

Eckhart says that as long as a person keeps his or her own will and thinks that their will is to satisfy the will of God, that person does not have the poverty of spirit needed for union with God.[5] The person who is poor in the most spiritual sense wills nothing, knows nothing, and wants nothing; simply put, that person is not driven by ego. According to Eckhart a God-seeker should be "so disinterested and untrammeled that he does not know what God is doing in him." That person should allow God to be hidden and rejoice in God's hiddenness because then God lives freely in the person.

The union between creator and creature is one of Eckhart's most strong and pervasive themes. This theme of unity is so strong that he was accused of heresy. But Eckhart did not quarrel with the institutional church, and he denied that he taught anything heretical. He claimed he had no desire to propose a truth different from what he believed to be inherent in Christianity, which was that God and soul are united. Because of the way he highlighted this unity of the divine and human, Eckhart gave a new vitality to the dry bones of doctrine, bringing alive the individual's sense of relationship with God.

What was regarded as threatening by church authorities was that Eckhart's teaching was taken to imply that the church as an institution, with priesthood and sacraments, might not be as essential as people were led to believe. For Eckhart, the issue was deeper. He saw that the most fundamental opening to God comes through trust in personal union with the hidden God. Eckhart challenged the believer to awaken to the presence of God within.

Eckhart's teaching on the unity of human beings and God, as radical as Christianity itself, was made more radical by his insistence that a person should be "empty of his own knowledge, as he was when he did not exist." Human beings are called to surrender in faith to the unity that is already present. Surrender means accepting the union with the divine that is human destiny without trying to define or explain it.

As for the pain of longing the seeker experiences when God feels out of reach, Eckhart offers a creative explanation. In seeking to know God, one sets desire high. This lofty desire can lead to even more intense desire. A person may feel frustrated because desire never seems to result in attainment. The soul, he says, is like a vessel that grows as it is filled. "If a bin able to hold a carload grew while you were dumping your load in it, you could never fill it. The soul is like that: the more it wants the more it is given; the more it receives the more it grows."[6] The capacity for God is not stable. The pain of longing seems to carve out a deepening capacity. Other mystics testify to this as well. Saint John of the Cross is one of them.

Saint John of the Cross provides us with a poetic vision of long-ing for a hidden God in his *Ascent of Mount Carmel* and *Dark Night of the Soul*.[7] John, a Spanish Carmelite, who, with Teresa of Avila, reformed the Carmelite Order, built on and modified the triple way of spiritual development. He saw the stages as a journey from a dark night of the senses to a dark night of the spirit as God continually calls the individual to spiritual development.

Purgation represents a dark night in which a person learns to quiet the desire for gratification. Illumination (or betrothal) signals another night when the individual comes to know the God to be fol-lowed, but obscurely. And the third stage of union (or spiritual mar-riage) draws the seeker of God into a night where God is known to be present in absence. John treasures the nights involved in these phases, the night of the senses and the night of the spirit, because through them a person draws closer to the God beyond feelings, images, and ideas.

Each of these stages has an active and a passive expression.[8] In the active night of the senses and the spirit, human activity domi-nates. In the passive night the divine element is predominant. In the active night of the senses, the individual focuses attention on prayer, good works, and discipline. In the active night of the spirit, she or he becomes aware of underlying spiritual values of prayerfulness rather than "saying prayers" and overcoming spiritual egocentrism in order to be more faithful and authentic.

In the passive night of the senses, a person recognizes the secret sources of spiritual pride that instill an insidious superiority. She or he is humbled by a realization of the stubborn roots of ego that pop up in the form of greed for spiritual experience or anger at another's lack of virtue. The individual feels powerless to alter the situation and becomes aware that only God can resolve the dilemma. In the passive night of the spirit, the God-seeker experiences the ultimate challenge to spiritual growth in the "loss" of the only God he or she knew. In this night all images and ideas of God seem empty and insufficient to lead to the mind to God. God is hidden in an unimaginable abyss.

John understands the deepening mystery of God as part of the spiritual maturing process. People expect a God they have been conditioned to expect. On the journey through darkness that God is not found. One must rely on faith, a faith that does not dispel the darkness but allows one to "see" in the dark. Because God is more deeply hidden than ever as a person enters the passive night of the spirit, there can be a profound sense of God's absence. Yet in some strange way, the feeling of the absence of God is felt to be pregnant with an inexpressible presence.

John sings of this presence and absence in his poem *The Dark Night*. In *The Dark Night*, the soul rejoices in the path to union with God through spiritual negation. John speaks of the soul leaving its house, its self, in secret, unobserved by anyone. The soul's only light and guide is the desire burning within. This inner light leads to "where there waited one who was to me well known, and in a place where no one came in view."

To the soul that finds itself here, the night is more desirable than the dawn because it leads to the Beloved by a path that suspends all the senses. The soul cannot be deceived because it no longer relies on intellect or senses. Human perception no longer obscures the true presence. It is a blessed night, which the lover would not exchange for a superficial encounter with the Beloved.

The austere spiritualities of the author of *The Cloud*, Eckhart, and John of the Cross seem demanding and even impossible. Of course, their approaches are not for everyone. They are most relevant for those who, despite continuing faithfulness to and longing for God, find themselves at an impasse. These authors reassure them that the impasse is an opportunity. Even those who do not feel anguish because of God's hiddenness have something to learn from these and other mystics.

Further Lessons from the Mystics

Besides the lessons the mystical writers teach us about the hidden God, we can also draw some pastoral conclusions from their work. The first lesson we can take from the mystics is not to expect that conventional and practical methods can simply be transferred to spiritual situations. Sometimes we try to build a relationship with God as we would manage any other project. We listen to the voices of practicality and reason. We allow our active energy and logic to lead the way. The God-human relationship calls for different skills, skills that put practical concerns aside—for a time.

There is a time for active and practical concerns, but the mystics remind us there is also a time to still our activity and listen to the spirit. Our bias for a certain kind of activity often prevents us from hearing a more subtle spiritual voice. The mystics urge us to listen to the wordless voice that arises from profound silence. They give us a glimpse of what it would look like if we could let go of the need to know God as we know other things and to be in control.

Mechthild of Magdeburg, a mystic of the thirteenth century, left an account of her relationship with God in *The Flowing Light of the Godhead*.[9] In this work Mechthild constructs a dialogue between the soul and the senses in which she converses about her need to suspend reliance on the senses. She testifies that her yearning to be one with the hidden God demands that she listen to her inner spiritual nature.

The voices of practicality, communicated through the senses, warn her not to go there. She will be swallowed up, in over her head, unable to function in ordinary life. The senses caution her not to abandon them as her most reliable source of knowledge. Mechthild replies that her desire for union must take her beyond the practicality of the senses. It is her nature to seek God above all else.

Like fish that cannot drown in water or birds that do not fall in air because they follow their nature, she too must follow hers. She assures the senses she will return to them when she must; they help her through many dangers. To encounter God, however, she must rely on a knowledge that is more intuitive and obscure.

Mechthild of Magdeburg accepted a role for the senses in practical matters, but when it came to God, she knew she must follow an intuition that did not depend on ordinary knowledge. She was able to accept that there are different means for different goals. We who live in a world obsessed with practicality and results can ponder her advice.

She and other mystics teach us the importance of knowing when to let go of practical concerns, which, at some points, can be useful in the spiritual life, but at others will not be. Bonaventure tells us that there is a phase in the life of the spirit when we need to exercise discipline to break the hold of bad habits and establish good ones. There is also a time when discipline will not help and we need to trust in God alone. Once the basic foundation and practice of faith are solid, we can relax our hold on what was necessary at an earlier stage. We can learn to trust ourselves to know when it is time to let go and dwell in the silence of God. The challenge is to learn to know ourselves well enough that we can be confident of this intuition.

There is another lesson to learn from the mystics: the importance of understanding the kind of growth we are called to at a given point. When are we being called to stretch and what impedes the spirit from expanding? Hidden resistances may blind us to this knowledge. We may fear the loss of our familiar God or distrust our ability to walk a different spiritual path. We may be blind to our illusions about God and self. Growth is slow and comes only when we are ready. We may not always know our own readiness. In this endeavor we are aided by the insight and wisdom of good guides who can help us to be honest and to move beyond what is safe and comfortable.

The mystics appreciated those whose gifts of spiritual wisdom could help them discern whether their instincts were to be trusted. Many mystics lived at a time when the spiritual life was taken seriously. Truly gifted counselors in their time were not always easy to find, but one could eventually find a trusted mentor, a skilled guide for greater spiritual self-knowledge and honesty in the quest for God. For us, it is often not so easy.

In our self-help society there are many who claim to teach self-knowledge. But the knowledge they promise may not bring us closer to God and others in honesty and humility. For that, we need to look for guides who do not offer easy answers, guides who will show that deep listening takes us farther than many words. These guides may not be mystics themselves, but they will teach us to respect the silence of deep listening that leads to genuine self knowledge—and knowledge of the hidden God.

Taking these lessons from the mystics, our task is to ponder how we will use what we have learned. On one hand, our challenge is to find our own God language that will keep us aware of God's hiddenness. On the other hand, our challenge is to discover what spiritual skills we need to continue to journey with a hidden God in a new spiritual landscape. These challenges will be taken up in Parts 2 and 3. But first, in light of what we have learned from all our spiritual ancestors about the hidden God, the concluding chapter of Part 1 offers an opportunity to consider how their spirit might guide our journey today.

6

Tracking the Elusive God Today

By now it is apparent that the hiddenness of God is not a new phenomenon. Many of our spiritual ancestors discovered God to be hidden more deeply in mystery than they imagined. From the Hebrew Scriptures through the Christian Scriptures, from the intellectual theologians to the poetic mystics, giants of spiritual wisdom have attested to the power of the hidden God who captured their hearts and imagination but who eluded their grasp.

Our struggles to relate to a hidden God are similar in some ways to those of our spiritual ancestors. We, too, find it difficult to continue to trust God in the face of the challenges of suffering, the absence of clear answers, the claims of different religions, and the hope of closeness while we sense distance or absence. We also discover new challenges in the twenty-first century because our context is so different from that of our ancestors.

The context for our difficulty with a hidden God is the surrounding world of technology and constant change, fragmentation and uncertainty, sensory overload and skepticism. These conditions compound the spiritual challenges we face because they stifle our capacity to live with mystery.

Even religious people are sometimes suspicious of talk about mystery. There is good reason to be wary. Talk of mystery can be an excuse for facing problems head on. It can prevent us from solving the problems that can be solved. It can also lead to preoccupation with rituals and esoteric knowledge that obscure the real importance of mystery. But there can be almost as much danger in avoiding mystery. When we fail to accept the presence of mystery in our lives, we lose the sense of wonder that keeps us humble. Most important, we miss the opportunity to deepen our relationship with God, who surpasses all we know or can imagine.

Part of the problem with mystery is the narrow way it is popularly defined. Many think of mystery as something like an illness whose cause is not known. They anticipate that if they try hard enough, eventually the mystery will disappear. A spiritual mystery is not like that. Spiritual mystery is so intrinsically mysterious that if the mystery were "removed," what it refers to would lose all meaning.[1] The nature of spiritual mystery is to remain a mystery.

Paul Tillich says that mystery, like revelation, is something hidden that "cannot be approached through ordinary ways of gaining knowledge." Appreciating mystery takes a way of seeing that is different from the ordinary sight of practical life. Tillich says with ordinary knowledge one has to open one's eyes to grasp meaning. Conversely, mystery requires a person to close his or her eyes because it transcends the act of seeing. At least, it requires persons to close their eyes to habitual ways of seeing.

Since our culture conditions us to ignore or dismiss mystery, we first need to reopen the door to the perception of mystery, at least a crack. There are several ways to do this. First, it helps to stop taking the ordinary for granted and to approach it as something unfamiliar. Then, it is useful to learn to hold the idea of mystery more lightly so that mystery becomes less ponderous. Finally, it is important to note that mystery is to be expected in a multi-dimensional world.

Seeing the Mysterious in the Ordinary

Throughout the history of the Judaeo-Christian tradition our spiritual ancestors journeyed with a hidden God. As they found their previous ways of seeing challenged, they realized God was more mysterious than they thought. They slowly had to let go of some of their preconceptions about God. The world in which they lived accepted mystery more readily than ours does, but that didn't make it any easier to see in their experience the promise of a new way of relating to God.

Living in an age of uncertainty, we too have to learn to relate to God in new ways that still respect the mystery of God. But we are so sure we understand the way things work that we much more easily miss the presence of mystery in the ordinary world. Artists have something to teach us about how to approach the ordinary world with a sense of wonder that fosters greater sensitivity to mystery.

Gifted artists see freshly, and in so doing they disorient us from our usual ways of perceiving. The artist takes some part of our world that habit has made dull and looks at it in a new way so that it becomes strange for us. The artist helps us to see as if for the first time. The artist de-familiarizes our familiar world.[2]

By de-familiarizing objects so that we have to look long and carefully at them, the artist forces us to really look instead of allowing us to rely on the habit of recognition. Claude Monet squinted to see the lily pads in his garden, and Georgia O'Keeffe stared at a petunia until it became larger than a tree. These visionaries make us blink in disbelief until we find ourselves seeing what we didn't see before. In sharing their vision, they open us up beyond the limits of our familiar habitual approaches.

In thinking of God, we often rely on the habit of recognition. We hear the word *God* and immediately conjure up a cluster of associations. Habitual ways of thinking can easily get in the way of truly seeing our relationship with God and the mystery in it. We need the eyes of an artist to discover a fresh view, a new perspective.

Artists, like the spiritually wise, see what is often veiled to the rest of us. If we compare an artist's rendition of a scene with our own perception or with a photograph, we are often amazed that they see the view through a different colored lens or with the light reflecting in a different way. It is even more instructive when an artist combines elements we would not have thought of combining or sees or releases the form hidden in a block of marble as Michelangelo did. Artists, including artists of the spirit, do something similar as they make the world unfamiliar and thus help us discover the richness obscured by our complacency.

Artists of the spirit are those people who, like our spiritual ancestors and like visual and performing artists, open doors of insight into a spiritual life hidden within us. Artists of the spirit may be ordinary people who inspire us to reconsider assumptions we routinely make about God. In an unself-conscious and spontaneous way, they make the familiar unfamiliar so that we are prodded to overcome habit and self-satisfaction. When we are locked into a vision of God that no longer reflects our spiritual experience, an artist of the spirit can unlock the imagination without negating the hiddenness of God.

It is important to preserve the hiddenness of God because the infinite God always transcends our limited understanding. Spiritual traditions have testified to this for centuries. However much these traditions have relied on words and images to convey their messages, they ultimately know the limits of mental constructs. So even though it is necessary to use words and images, it is important to remain humble about the limits of all human expressions about God in order to know there is not just one way to speak of God.

Artists know there is not just one way to present their subjects. And they know they are giving expression to something that is not obvious. Paul Klee, who created his works early in the twentieth century, said that the role of the artist is not to present what is already visible, but to make visible what is invisible.

Believers today can try to develop an artist's eye so they do not have to rely overly on secondhand language and images. If they lack the skills for that, then it would help to develop an appreciation for the work of artists of the spirit around them—writers, spiritual guides, activists, ordinary faithful—who make visible a reality that the rest of us are likely to miss. If these artists are successful, their vision stretches the mind and puts us just slightly off balance. They help us pay attention.

There are many artists of the spirit who can instruct us. Some are professionals who earn a livelihood from their work. Others show they have an artist's eye by the creative way they live their lives and think about their faith. Among them are some who teach us to hold the idea of mystery more lightly.

Holding Mystery More Lightly

Most of us do not find the time to reflect on our ideas of God so that we can recognize new possibilities. It is easier to accept the images and ideas that we inherited, especially those that insist on omnipotence or omniscience. This language often paralyzes us in a stilted reverence we no longer feel (but sometimes wish we did). The attributes replace mystery, making God more remote. A lighter approach to mystery could help.

The writer Nancy Mairs knows how important it is to recognize the dangers of speaking of God with deadly seriousness about getting it right. Mairs observes that once we say the word *God*, God goes stiff as a corpse.[3] Precise terms can never nail God down; God remains elusive despite our best and most careful efforts to be theologically correct. Mairs admits she can't avoid God language, but she dismantles some of the solid concepts and images that try to speak too definitively of God. "Just as a wave, at the instant of observation, collapses into a particle, at the moment of utterance, God coalesces and freezes." The word *God* embodies a fragment of meaning, but never enough. Mairs describes her own movement toward a freer attitude about God.

Mairs talks about losing her early image of the "Daddy God." She says it is not so much that God disappeared but rather that God let her go. What disappeared is an imaginative picture of God that kept her tied to need, desire, and fear, as well as the hope that the world would be changed to make her happy. She did not decide to change her attitude about this image. The image changed when the relationship shifted and freed her from unhealthy dependencies. She can now joke somewhat irreverently about God getting older, grayer, and a little deaf to her demands, to her relief. She knows that the images she uses now are no more the reality than the ones she held earlier. Instead of approaching God with the gravity of one who is going to set the world straight by giving us the real story of who God is, Mairs simply lightens up and lets us know she accepts her lack of knowledge about God. In making this shift, Mairs opens the door to discovering the God beyond words who is at the heart of spiritual life.

In taking our ideas of God too seriously, we constrict our spirituality. We ignore the incongruities and ambiguities that are part not only of the mystery of God but also of the mystery we are to ourselves. These incongruities and ambiguities point to new possibilities and opportunities. There will always be gaps and inconsistencies in our understanding of God and ourselves. We can lament the absence of perfect coherence or we can hold the absence lightly and let it carry us on.

Holding our beliefs and spirituality more lightly can be both honest and freeing. Instead of tracking the elusive God with heavy steps, we might learn to tread softly, respectful of how much is outside our view. Holding our ideas of God more lightly can give us a humbler attitude toward ourselves and our spiritual aspirations.

Annie Dillard illustrates this in an essay called "An Expedition to the Pole."[4] In this essay she muses about our movement toward the inaccessible God. Dillard reflects on the Pole of Relative Inaccessibility, the "imaginary point on the Arctic Ocean farthest from land in any direction." This is not a literal point, but it is a way to speak of our inability to grasp the transcendent God. The Absolute or God "is that point of spirit farthest from every accessible point of spirit in all directions." In a flight of imagination, Dillard sets out mentally in solitude and silence toward the Via Negativa, "the lightless edge where the slopes of knowledge dwindle, and love, for its own sake, lacking an object, begins."

Dillard imagines herself traveling through seasons of solitude until she lands on an ice floe where a small group huddles. These unlikely companions float on together, singing and amusing one another. They are the church, a motley group of all ages and types who are also headed for the pole of relative inaccessibility. They are as improbable a group as any to strive for such a daunting goal. But they are drawn by a mystery more powerful than their limits. Dillard sees herself as one of them. Dillard senses that we do not move alone in our quest for God, but are part of a body of seekers. Moving toward the elusive God is not just a solitary project—it is a project of love (of neighbor as well as God).

At the same time, Dillard feels the journey that takes us beyond the edges of ordinary knowledge is one that sometimes seems too much for us. In an essay called "Total Eclipse" Dillard considers how she and other observers at an eclipse, though they were fascinated by the uncanny experience, nevertheless started back to their cars before the eclipse was over. Dillard observes how they turned even from the "depths of mystery" and the "heights of splendor," and hurried back for the familiar. A brush with the supernatural, when we are not ready to entertain it, may end with a sigh of relief.

These are strange images she offers, not designed to replace the traditional images of creed and worship, but calculated to jolt us out of habitual modes of thought. She hints, as others do, that we do not know what we are talking about when we say *God* though we are often sure we do. Eckhart Tolle makes a similar point. He says the word *God* has been emptied of its meaning because of centuries of misuse.[5] He explains that people who have never considered the vast depth behind the word, or reverenced a sense of the sacred, use it with the utter confidence that they know what it means. Some argue against it with the same conviction. As soon as the word is uttered, however, Tolle says it becomes a closed concept.

Mairs and Dillard break the hold of the closed concept of God and put a helpful strangeness back into our metaphors for God. We need to find our own strange metaphors for God, new images that subvert the certainty of the closed concept and remind us we are dealing with a God of mystery who abides in a relational world.

Mystery in a Multi-dimensional World

Complexity is part of the fabric of life. The simplest and most ordinary experience is layered with many dimensions because it is part of an interconnected and relational world. It doesn't make sense to continue to speak of God or the will of God as if it had no relation to the organic, interconnected universe. When we simplify our view of God so much that we deny complexity, we eliminate genuine mystery.

Alfred North Whitehead cautioned against trying to simplify our ideas of God to deal with the spiritual crisis the modern world is facing.[6] He saw the dangers in reducing religion to a few ideas that produce pleasing emotions and agreeable conduct. Such simplification would not likely lead to spiritual truth in the long run but would tend to become blind to its own one-sidedness. Instead of trying to articulate a view of God that reassures us of order and certainty, we would do better to admit we do not understand just how God moves amidst the broad complexity of life.

Complexity has always been part of religion's richness. Even metaphors that appear straightforward have multiple layers of meaning and paradox. One that illustrates the complex multiple presences of God is the image of host and guest, a familiar biblical theme. In the Hebrew Scriptures God is presented from time to time through the image of host or guest. In Genesis, God appears in the guise of strangers looking for hospitality. In the twenty-third psalm God sets a table for the psalmist in the midst of enemies.

In the Christian Scriptures Jesus uses the theme of host and guest in a variety of ways. He speaks of the reign of God as a feast where the faithful are guests. He speaks of God as the host who feeds thousands by multiplying loaves and fishes and as one who gives a great dinner to which many are invited. What is interesting and indicative of the potential complexity of the image, however, is the way the roles of host and guest shift and are interchangeable at times.

In Matthew's Gospel Jesus describes the faithful ones at the last judgment as being host to God who is present but hidden in the lowliest and most needy. When these merciful ones give a cup of water to a person in need, when they feed the hungry and clothe the naked, when they invite those to table who cannot repay them, it is not always clear who is host and who is guest. Is the recipient of this generosity the guest or is it the true host in disguise? The line between host and guest blurs, but it isn't really necessary to make it clear.

A complex image like the guest-host throws us off balance. From time to time, this can be a good thing. It can restore the tension characteristic of all metaphorical speech about God, a tension that serves as a vivid reminder of the hidden God. Images with more than one dimension can keep us from relying on a few simple metaphors for God that lull us into forgetting that God is mystery and that dull us to new forms of God's presence.

We don't have to decide when our views of God need to change. The impetus for change in our vision of God and in our relationship with God comes from entering into new situations of religious and moral complexity. As we have seen from our spiritual ancestors who had to confront new situations, holding on to simplistic images is not the best strategy. New situations can reawaken us to the presence of mystery hinted at in the many dimensions of experience. In Part 2, we will explore some images of God that are multi-dimensional and that stretch the imagination while preserving the hiddenness of God.

II

Exploring Images of God

7

The Problem of Naming God

In the preceding chapter, we explored the need for images of God that stretch the imagination and are multi-dimensional. Gregory the Great provides a clue to this type of image in his description of Scripture. Gregory writes that Scripture is shallow enough for a bird to wade in and deep enough for an elephant to swim in. The bird needs just enough water to satisfy its limited desires, while the elephant, because of its great size, needs something different. The river of Scripture is diverse and vast enough for each to meet its needs. But its depth and breadth are greater than any one individual's capacity.

This metaphor of Scripture as a deep river of wisdom has sustained God-seekers through the ages. It is the kind of metaphor that can also guide those who are looking to name God today. The images that we use to name God ought to be simple enough to satisfy those who are not inclined to probe deeply and, at the same time, complex enough to consistently engage those who are.

In addition to the challenge of finding images that are multi-dimensional, we are also challenged to find images that speak to us within our own unique culture. When the only images of God we can imagine are better suited to another culture or age, it will be harder for us to relate to the God they present. Likewise, when we outgrow an image of God that had personal meaning for us at an earlier stage of our lives, God may seem less relevant. In such cases the problem is not God but a particular image of God. The solution to this problem is not to give up on belief in God completely but to allow our ideas of God to be transformed.

When Thomas Merton spoke of the disappearance of the familiar God in our age, he warned that this experience should not send people back to the God of their childhood. Merton encouraged us to face the challenges of spiritual development within our culture and within ourselves with courage and faith. While he didn't speak much of the influence of culture on the choice of God images, it is a matter of concern for us as we come to realize how much culture affects our attitude toward particular views of God.[1]

Ways of Naming God

Some of the most powerful images we have used for God have been images of relationship. We speak of God as Creator, Ruler, Judge, or Father among other things. Each of these suggests a particular kind of relationship. One may suggest power, another may suggest compassion, and still another generosity. We can grow so used to one particular image of God that we forget how much that image has been influenced by culture to start with and how much it may be affected by changes in culture. Culture should not dictate which images we use, but it is hard to ignore the influence it has on images of God and on our attitude toward them.

Particular religious images and analogies tell us something about the attitudes of a culture toward certain relationships. Every culture, including a religious culture such as the church, values certain kinds of relationships. When conditions change, and the culture or individuals start to embrace new values, attitudes toward familiar images of relationship may change.

In the last three or four centuries, human beings' approach to God has undergone tremendous change, related in part to changes in Western culture. For example, the God who spoke primarily through the Bible and the church must now be seen as speaking in other ways as well because reliance on authority, in a variety of forms, has lessened. People look more to their own experience for religious understanding, instead of the testimony of those in official positions. An understanding of God that relied heavily on images of authority has given way to a vision of God that draws on other kinds of relationships.

Our attitude toward God's functions has also changed. In the past God was often understood to "do" what a powerful hierarchical figure would do, and human beings responded accordingly. The power associated with a hierarchical God no longer evokes the same response. The image of God as king whose every word must be obeyed fails to inspire people who live in societies where such unquestioning obedience is not desirable. The image of God as paternalistic father who always steps in to make things right falls short in an age when people are brought up to assume responsibility as adults. The image of God as judge who requires one particular response to a moral challenge diminishes as people today face more complex moral situations. In short, images that promote hierarchical functions seem out of touch with the way people understand themselves and the way their world functions.

A hierarchical God reigns over a world that is organized according to rank or levels of importance. Images of God as Lord, King, Ruler, Judge, Creator, Father—all suggest that God is a powerful figure who relates to human beings who are dependent and subservient. Their primary response is expected to be obedience and allegiance. The hierarchical images used for God do not leave much room for ambiguity or paradox.

When we live in a world where hierarchy no longer controls thought, and we struggle with moral issues that have no precedent, we pay less attention to hierarchical images of God. The God who expects us to "know our place" and behave accordingly has yielded to a God who challenges and supports us in our struggle to act justly.

As we move away from hierarchical images of God toward images that reflect a different kind of relationship, we enter a dark zone. Old images and ways of naming God slip into the background before others rise to replace them. Our expectations of God become vague or confused. During this transitional time, familiar images may not be as compelling as they once were. We may think they are the only images that can be associated with God because we are unaware of less common images such as Wisdom or Mystery. Since the God most of us are familiar with is associated with conventional religion, the institution and traditions of religion may begin to seem irrelevant.

Conventional religion offers rules, doctrines, practices, and images that are useful in some cultures or at some stages, but not at others. At times of far-reaching social or personal change, the thought patterns and language of conventional religion cannot always keep pace with change. New images of God arise, but slowly. The old images need not be discarded because they can often be transformed, but before that can happen believers must often swim in deeper waters of faith where it is not always possible to name God easily.

Naming Relationships with God

All relationships are a challenge to understand and name, not only because they are mysteries but also because we bring different attitudes and capacities to them. Martin Buber's seminal work *I and Thou* focuses on two basic attitudes that can affect our relationship with others and with God. One is the attitude in which we relate to the other by standing outside the relationship, a stance that allows us to analyze and name it. This is the I-It relation. The other is the attitude of absorption in the relationship prior to thinking about it. This is the I-Thou relation.[2]

Both attitudes are involved in all our dealings with the world and with God, but when the I-It relationship dominates, as it often does in day-to-day activities, the focus is on experiencing things and situations. An I-It relationship attends more to aspects of experience rather than to the whole relationship. I-It describes an attitude that allows us to treat God as a separate entity we can objectify and name; it allows us to talk *about* God. It cannot capture how it is to be in the midst of a relationship.

An I-It relationship uses words or ideas that make reality into an object. Whenever we talk about God, God becomes an object, as if God were one being among other beings. God is not a being among other beings, but infinite Being Itself which cannot be objectified. When we approach a relationship perceiving the other as an object, we are aware of our separateness. We perceive ourselves as the subject, the conscious knower. And we perceive the other as *other*, as an objectified one we can try to understand, can evaluate, can relate to as sympathetic or unsympathetic to our interests. Even when we have strong personal feelings about the other, if we think, compare, or seek, we are relating to the other as "it," whether the other is God or not.

The I-It dimension of relationships makes us aware of difference or separation and creates a dualism. As long as we think and act only out of the awareness of our unique individuality, we will perceive a chasm between ourselves and the elusive God. When we are able to forget self, which makes us separate, we can simply dwell in the I-Thou aspect of the relationship without having to define, analyze, defend, or even seek it. In an I-Thou relationship dualism evaporates.

Buber says that when people confront another as Thou, they do not perceive that other as one among an array of beings, but perceive the relationship in its wholeness without discriminating. To be present to another as Thou is to make oneself present to the presence of the other.

An I-Thou attitude disposes a person for contact with the living God rather than with an idea of God. I-Thou is the attitude of contemplative prayer in which one faces God directly (and is faced by God) instead of merely using "appropriate" prayer language. True encounter with God does not lend itself to the language we ordinarily use to speak of God. To speak of God at all, we must fall back on I-It language. That is the hazard of all speech about God.

I and Thou, steeped in Buber's Judaism, attempts to get back to the roots of biblical faith in the Word. The revelation of God's name to Moses, "I will be who I will be," is the relational name of God before it turns into an objective name. Wholehearted listening to God, prior to I-It language and the naming of God, precedes whatever we want to say about God. At this level dualism is avoided.

We slip into attitudes of dualism over and over. Life must be a rhythm of I-It and I-Thou relations, because we cannot function in an unending I-Thou attitude. We must carry on our daily affairs earning a living, fulfilling our responsibilities, planning for the future—even devoting ourselves to the management of our personal relations. We cannot avoid the world of I-It. But the cultural environment we live in one-sidedly favors I-It relations. If we follow culture unthinkingly, we are the poorer for it. If we let I-It dominate our spiritual life, we will be able to engage in religious activities but will not meet the living God who can be personally known only in an immediate relationship.

Martin Buber has pointed out how our attitude toward relationship is much more important than how we name it. Yet even he named the relationship with God, though with great care to preserve its mystery. So, too, if we try to name God, the hiddenness of God should be present in our naming. One way to do this is to give greater attention to paradox, which prevents us from reducing God to a simple idea capable of being expressed in I-It language. Jesus often relied on paradox to show a way to a deeper and more authentic relationship with God as Thou.

Jesus—A Guide for Relating to God

Mark, as well as Matthew and Luke, tells the story of a man who asks Jesus how to gain eternal life (10:17–22). As he often does, Jesus puts it back to him. "You know the commandments. You shall not commit adultery; You shall not murder. . . ." The man replies that he has kept the commandments since his youth. Then Jesus tells him there is still one thing lacking. He needs to sell everything, give the money to the poor, and follow Jesus. But the man becomes sad because he is very rich, and he leaves without following Jesus. Jesus says that it is easier for a camel to pass through the eye of a needle than for a rich person to be saved. Was Jesus saying something only about the danger of riches? Or was he also suggesting something important about being in relationship with God?

Each of the accounts of this story concludes with the disciples asking who can be saved if it is so difficult for someone who is rich. The rich man must have wondered about this himself. According to the conventional religious wisdom of the time, wealth is a sign of God's favor. The rich are blessed by God for living a godly life. The rich man, therefore, might have been quite surprised to learn that riches were getting in the way of a fuller spiritual life.

There is also another kind of wealth Jesus is asking this man to relinquish. It is the "wealth" of his religious status. The rich man has religious status because his knowledge and observance of the commandments and the Mosaic Law supposedly put him in a special relationship with God. This knowledge gives him moral and religious superiority. Yet he senses that this is not enough and asks what he must do to gain eternal life. Jesus' answer that he must give up his wealth (including his social and religious wealth) puts him in the position of having to let go of his customary way of identifying himself in relation to God. He did not expect to have to surrender this.

The rich man could not have imagined he had to let go of something that gave him meaning and identity. He could not have imagined being asked to empty himself of what he held to be religious truth in order to give himself to God's truth that surpasses understanding. In being asked to let go of what he considered to be God's blessings, he would have to get his sense of worth from his relation to God alone. This was more than he could comprehend.

As devout as the man appeared to be, in some ways he had been engaged in an I-It relationship with God. Religious observance had been the measure of this relationship. Jesus did not disparage this. After all, he first told him to obey the commandments. But once it was clear he had a firm foundation, Jesus invited him to a relationship with God in which religious knowledge and practices were no longer to be the main focus. God was to be the focus. To make God the focus, Jesus directs him to give up one kind of riches for much greater riches.

This is the way of paradox: loss will become gain. This is the way of mystery: God is hidden but will become known when we stop seeking the God we think we know. The problem of naming God is that it requires surrender to the mystery of a God who cannot be defined. To respect the mystery, we look at our efforts to find more adequate names for God not as attempts to make definitive statements but as experiments that seek to uncover new dimensions of our relationship with God.

The Value of Paradox in Naming God

The challenge of learning a new name for God is daunting. The rich young man who approached Jesus discovered that. When Jesus invited him to sell everything and follow him, he was inviting him to live at the edges of his customary way of seeing things. The young man wasn't ready then to live such an unsettling religious existence. Jesus did not tell him to give up his religious convictions any more than Jesus himself gave up Judaism and the religious traditions he inherited. Jesus asked the man instead to trust the intuition that impelled him to seek more, the intuition that lies beneath the beliefs that were handed down to him. The rich young man was invited to inhabit a new spiritual landscape, where the name of God would be revealed through his personal encounter with God.

It seems that we, too, are at the horizon of a new spiritual landscape. We sense there is more to God than the God we knew in the past. We have an opportunity to learn to perceive the presence of God anew, but we need to be careful not to try to make God more visible than is possible. We need to remember we are trying to name the Unnamable, to make comprehensible the One we cannot comprehend. We are trying to speak of what we perceive only darkly.

On this journey we are carrying the baggage of names and images that have grown so familiar and so taken for granted that they can sometimes substitute for the relationship. Words are reassuring, but they mislead us into thinking we can access God the way we access anything else. Most of us think, even religiously, with an I-It mind. A relationship with God, like other relationships, carries its fullest meaning when we can stop to let ourselves be addressed by Thou. When we do turn back, as we eventually must, from the attitude of I-Thou to speak of relationship with God in I-It language, we need language that will preserve the mystery of I-Thou. Paradoxical language moves us in that direction.

Paradoxes don't make sense to those who are accustomed only to using linear or I-It thinking. An approach to God that includes paradox can also be frustrating for those with a low tolerance for ambiguity or apparent contradiction. Paradoxes do not offer a neat and clear formula for who God is. They do not give the reassurance that conventional religious ideas give. So it will be tempting to avoid images of God that are paradoxical and to wade among hints of God's mystery. By wading, however, we draw back from the depths of meaning.

To probe the depths of God's hiddenness we need images that demand more of us, images that require us to give up our expectations that God should meet our intellectual and emotional needs. These will often be paradoxical images that stretch our capacity for new levels of relationship and allow us to perceive diverse aspects of God simultaneously. God can be felt as absent yet also somehow present, as loving yet challenging, as formidable and yet compassionate. In place of the simplicity of a God who is either majestic *or* comforting, we may find a God who is both majestic and humble, comforting and challenging, powerful and vulnerable. Such paradoxical visions of God stretch the mind and imagination. They also remind us dramatically that the fullness of God remains hidden behind the names we use.

If we wish to do justice to the hidden presence, we must speak with a reverence for the dark and illuminating expansiveness of God. The mystics often spoke of the dark mystery of God, but for them the mystery is never darkness alone. It is paradoxically another form of light. To appreciate light and dark in the hidden God, it helps to grow more accepting of paradox. Paradoxes draw us into the hidden places of the heart full of new invitations to spiritual growth. They introduce us to a oneness that is much more complex and multi-layered than the kind of unity we usually imagine.

We have seen mystics use images that suggest the borders of human knowledge — night, the cloud of unknowing, nothingness. These images are effective in reminding us of the limits of our knowledge of God, but we also need images that will reflect the positive and intuitive dimensions of knowledge that surface when God's presence is felt powerfully. That is why we need not abandon images totally, but instead need to find images that preserve the elements of both affirmation and negation.

In the next several chapters, I explore some paradoxical images of God that can widen our perspective on God. They are images that remind us that for every aspect of God that captures something of who God is, there is another that reveals a different, sometimes conflicting, aspect. The three images of God I have selected as revelatory of the mystery of our relationship with God are God as challenging companion, compassionate adversary, and fertile emptiness. These paradoxical names for God take us along less traveled paths where God may surprise us.

8

God as Challenging Companion

The image of God as Companion is such a familiar and comforting analogy for God that we rarely consider the fullness of its meaning. We assume we know all about what kind of presence is involved when we speak of a companion. Seldom do we consider conflicting and challenging elements in a companion relationship, especially when the companion is God.

When the image of God as Companion is taken one-dimensionally, it easily turns into a cozy, if not trite, way to reassure ourselves that there is a power in the universe that supports us and confirms our place in the center of our world. We can easily turn the image of companion into a projection of our own needs. To avoid misusing the image, it helps to take a closer look at its basic meaning and at its less obvious dimensions.

According to the origin of the word, companion means one who eats bread with another. Usage has extended its meaning to refer to one who lives with or travels with another. At face value, the term companion calls to mind a simple reassuring presence that remains with us, in more or less the same way, no matter what the situation. But that is not the full picture.

Though at first glance the idea of God as Companion appears simple and affirming, the relationship between companions can be as textured as a tapestry. While it is true that companions support us physically, emotionally, and spiritually, they may be challenging as well as supportive. Though they alleviate our loneliness, their absence can make us feel lonelier. As much as companions may be intimate friends, they may feel like strangers when their views or actions

contradict our preferences and remind us that they are not exten-
sions of ourselves.

It is also easy to consider the idea of companionship as a special
relationship between two particular persons without reference to anyone else. But each companion is part of a network of relations. So the
image of God as companion suggests something more than a personal
relationship; it hints at a web of connections that includes diverse people who are sometimes at odds with one another. Admitting these
connections not only makes the image more complex; it also discourages us from living only in our own comfort zone. The image of God
as companion reminds us to see ourselves in community with a companioning God and suggests many forms of God's presence.

Even something as basic as presence turns out to be multi-faceted.
When we do not feel God's presence as tangibly as we expect to, we
begin to speak of the companion God as absent. Presence and absence
appear to be opposites. This one-dimensional approach does not capture the richness and mutuality of a companion relationship where
presence and absence may not be mutually exclusive, but may co-exist.

The analogy of God as Companion has dimensions of mutuality
and paradox that present opportunities as well as challenges. There
are opportunities in a companion relationship for mutual enrichment
and the stretching of mental horizons, and there are challenges to
comfortable patterns and familiar controls. If one is willing to face
both opportunities and challenges, the companion relationship can
move one to new levels of relationship.

A relationship changes from time to time. Feelings of intimacy
intensify and wane. Presence and absence alternate. Companions
challenge one another sometimes even as they are affirming. We can
attune ourselves to the fullness of this image we use to speak of God
by looking at various dimensions of human companionship.

Dimensions of the Companion Relationship

Granted that the companion image remains limited as any
metaphor for God is limited, nevertheless it provides a fruitful analogy because it is rooted in a fundamental human experience. To come

to appreciate the image and experience more fully, however, we have to consider some of its many dimensions—its mutual give-and-take, its fluidity, its challenges, and its levels of intensity. Exploring these dimensions puts us on the path toward greater respect for the hidden presence of a companion God.

Companion is a term that suggests levels of mutuality layered within the apparently simple situation of "being with" one another. Because of mutual influence, it isn't always easy to know who guides the relationship. I watched a couple in the parking lot outside my window. She was shuffling along with the help of a wheeled walker, while he walked backward about twenty feet ahead of her. She trudged along for a dozen steps and stopped. He stopped. She adjusted the tubes in her nose that helped her to breathe. He gestured with a broad sweep of his arm. He began again to walk backward, and she followed for a dozen more steps.

Together they walked around the lot, repeating their pattern of steps, pauses, and gestures. Sometimes she increased the number of steps between pauses; sometimes she lessened them. Sometimes he let her rest longer. It was hard to tell who was leading and who following in this dance.

They created the steps of the dance together as they walked, since there was no pre-set choreography. If she balked at times, or if he grew impatient that she didn't try harder, that was part of the dance. What could be seen were the steps and the direction in which they were moving; what could not be seen was the mutuality they had worked out over the course of their lives together. They had learned to fine-tune their responses to one another. Their mutual give-and-take made it possible to maintain a companioning presence that was dynamic and always new.

The "walker waltz" could only happen between companions so present to each other that leading and following were one. There may be a lesson there about God's companioning presence. The metaphor of the dance suggests that we may not be able to know clearly when God is leading and when God is following. Would we look for different images of God if we thought God doesn't just lead but also follows?

The intuition that God follows as well as leads has been explored by the poet Karl Shapiro. In his poem "The 151st Psalm," Shapiro imagines the God of the Jewish people as an immigrant: God is constantly on the move because God's people are constantly on the move.[1]

The name of the poem gives a clue to Shapiro's new vision. There are 150 formally collected psalms in the Hebrew Scriptures, most of which reflect God's role as leader. Shapiro presents God in different light in "The 151st Psalm." Here, God is not so clearly identifiable as leader but is seen as one who must sometimes follow when the people are cast into situations or places where they do not yet find God.

The Jewish people have often been immigrants, dispersed by those who want them to be somewhere else. Shapiro sees their movement in history as the reversal of traditional imagery. Instead of being led to a permanent place of safety, they are still looking for a place to call home. Instead of seeing God in a pillar of fire that leads them, they see God as a pillar of fire that follows.

Shapiro's role reversal for God also shows a shift in God's power. God is no longer the powerful companion, the only one who leads; the Immigrant God leaves a power in the hands of the people. They beckon God to go with them, as they need the presence of God to continue the journey. God becomes a companion who adjusts to their movement. Shapiro closes "The 151st Psalm" with a prayer and an invitation to God, the companion who is both ancient and young, to follow the people.

The analogy of companion reveals its fluidity when viewed from different perspectives such as leading and following. A companion relationship also appears fluid when we look at the interplay of presence and absence. Presence and absence may be seen as two more faces of relationship.

A week or so after I first saw the couple from my window, I saw them walking arm in arm as she used only a quad cane. Still later I saw her one day slowly walking alone and unaided. He was physically present when she lacked strength, but not when she could do for herself. He moved with her when she needed physical and emotional assurance; she moved on her own when she had been strengthened by his companion support. He was somehow present in his absence.

The ability to accept physical and even spiritual absence can, paradoxically, be the impetus for a personal transformation. Sooner or later most of us have to find this out the hard way when we lose someone we love and suddenly realize that in some strange way the person is still with us. That person has changed who we are. Beloved companions become so much a part of our life that when they are not physically present, their absence is felt as an amputee feels the presence/absence of a limb. Even when they are absent, we experience both "absence" and another kind of "presence."

The followers of Jesus discovered this more expansive understanding of a companion relationship as they matured spiritually. After relating to him as an authoritative teacher who instructed them, they grew to experience him as an intimate friend. After knowing him through his physical presence, they came to know him after his death through his presence in absence. As his companion presence was transformed, so were theirs.

The Transformation of Companion Presence

In the first three gospels, Jesus' followers are clearly disciples. He is the teacher; they are the students. He instructs his followers in how to recognize the kingdom, how to pray, and what it means to be blessed. In the fourth gospel, John's gospel, another focus is added. John reveals Jesus as the unique companion of God and human beings.

The opening of the fourth gospel speaks of the Word of God as a tangible presence among human beings. It says that the Word of God became flesh in Jesus and dwelt in the midst of the human community; still further, it shows that Jesus knows God intimately in a way that other human beings are to discover themselves. Jesus teaches not only by words and actions but also by embodying the presence of God, which invites human friendship with God.

Jesus tells his disciples they should understand what he is telling them because it is not merely as a teacher that he has revealed himself. In his last talk with them before he dies, after he has washed their feet, he reveals they have become his friends. "I do not call you servants any longer because the servant does not know what the master is doing; but I have called you friends, because I have made known to you everything that I have heard from the Father." To be a companion is to know as a friend knows. Because they are his friends, they are in a privileged position to know God. But they often fail to learn from his example and even miss what he is telling them.

Jesus does not accept his followers' misunderstanding without confronting them. As a true friend, he doesn't dismiss their denseness with a shrug and sigh, thinking they may eventually figure out what he has been trying to say. Instead he challenges them to love one another, to know themselves better, and to pay attention. He gives them a new commandment that stretches their understanding of companionship.

The new commandment that Jesus leaves to his disciples—to love one another as he has loved them—flows from their relationship with him. They are not simply to adhere to his instruction; they are to exercise a ministry of service that embodies what it means to be a companion and a friend.

As a friend, Jesus loves his followers with boundless patience and forgiveness. As a sign of this love he gives them the instruction, in example, to serve one another as he does, symbolized in the washing of feet. At first Simon Peter refuses to allow Jesus to do this because he does not really grasp how this friendship is to be integrated into his life. Even when he agrees to it, he does not yet fully understand. Later he will. After the death of Jesus he will grasp that he is to love others as Jesus loves them, forgiving without limit and regarding no service as too menial.

Jesus also challenges his followers to know themselves. When Simon Peter promises he would lay down his life for Jesus, Jesus asks Peter to consider whether he really will. Jesus tells Peter he will betray him before dawn. Jesus' insight into Peter's character goes much further than Peter's own self-understanding. If Peter is to learn from Jesus' compassionate forgiveness, he will have to understand his weakness far better than he does. But the challenge Jesus presents is not heavy-handed and self-righteous. It is the challenge of a friend who hopes his friend will come to see the truth that will make him free.

The challenge to greater self-knowledge is related to another invitation to spiritual growth, capacity for really seeing and listening. At the time of Jesus' last conversation with the group, Jesus has been with his friends for some time. They have had an opportunity not only to listen but also to observe his exemplification of what he has taught. Yet Philip asks Jesus to show them the Father so they will be satisfied. Jesus responds, "Have I been with you all this time, Philip, and you still do not know me? Whoever has seen me has seen the Father." If God is still hidden to Philip, so is the message and meaning of Jesus. Jesus, the companion and friend, challenges Philip to really see and listen to what is before him.

These marks of a challenging companion—the invitations to love one another, to know themselves better, and to pay attention—show the risks and lessons of companionship, especially as it is transformed into friendship. In addition, Jesus has a last lesson to teach his friends so they can face the loss of his presence in death. It is to trust that he will be present even in his absence.

In John's Gospel just before his death Jesus tells his followers that when he is gone the Holy Spirit will be with them as a different kind of presence. How this presence will be experienced they cannot know in advance. So they cannot make the transition from relating to his physical presence to another kind of presence until they live through his absence. This is their final challenge as his friends.

After his death, the companions and friends of Jesus discover that the Spirit of God is a consoling and challenging presence just as Jesus was to them in his life. They find creative ways to share that presence in preaching, teaching, and service. As they learn how to respond to the new presence of the Spirit, they become a challenging and consoling companion presence to others.

The testimony of Scripture—John's gospel in particular—shows that slowness of understanding is not an insurmountable obstacle to attaining friendship with God. Like any close relationship, friendship takes time to ripen. Its evolution depends on willingness to grow into acceptance of the opportunities presented by a challenging companion.

The Evolution of Friendship

The analogy of friendship implies a greater degree of mutuality and understanding than that of companion. A friend is a *favored* companion, who is known, liked, and trusted. A friend is one whose values are understood and respected. The vast difference between God and ourselves, not to mention God's hiddenness, makes it difficult to imagine ourselves as a friend to God in a relationship of mutuality. But if we see friendship as growing and deepening, as a response to an invitation to friendship, friendship with God may not seem impossible after all. A human friendship between two people with significant differences sheds some light on this.

Martha Manning, a clinical psychologist and author, found herself searching for a way to reconnect with a world larger than herself after coming out of a period of depression.[2] After procrastinating for a while, Manning responded to a plea from the Arlington Homeless Shelter to become a "Santa" to a struggling family one Christmas. She doubted that she was in shape to help anyone, but she called the shelter and got the wish list of a local family—a single mother and three children.

As soon as Manning spoke with the mother, she realized that Raina was black. Since Martha is white, she feared she could be cast in the role of lily-white benefactor doling out gifts. This initial contact highlighted their differences in race and class. Martha discovered another difference that she felt was even more significant. It was the difference in their attitudes toward religion. Raina is a woman with a devout Christian faith. Martha often writes herself off as a "lapsed Catholic heathen."

In their initial conversation they worked out an arrangement for the delivery of the Christmas gifts. Once they got beyond their awkwardly polite beginning, the two women began to call each other occasionally. Martha and her husband Brian baby-sat for Raina's children once in a while. The women eventually went out to dinner, and despite their differences they developed a genuine appreciation for one another.

Through these exchanges, Martha and Raina came to know each other better. Because the story is told from Martha's perspective, we learn mostly how it affected her. Martha, the well-educated professional, entered into the world of the single mother who saves up quarters for the laundry and yearns for a decent home of her own. She sees what it is like to spend considerable time in a social world where she is in the minority. Yet she is welcomed into that world, and she and her husband become "aunt" and "uncle" to Raina's children. She realizes mutuality is possible even where there are differences.

What contributes most to the deepening of their friendship is the terminal illness of one of Raina's twin sons. Deven is diagnosed with a stage-four neuroblastoma at the age of three. He undergoes surgery, chemotherapy, and stem-cell transplants. Martha and Brian are there through it all. When Deven dies at the age of five, they mourn his loss as part of his extended family.

On the anniversary of Deven's death, Raina's family and Martha and Brian visit the cemetery. There they remember him and sing together at the grave, "Jesus Loves Me." Then Raina sings it alone, prayerfully and plaintively, as she did for her sick child in the middle of the night. Martha, the "heathen," allows the faith of Deven's mother to touch the ache in her own heart. She writes that, to her, Raina does more than sing. Raina ministers to them as she did to Deven.

As Deven was dying, Martha had prayed despite her own fractured faith. Now she enters into her friend's prayer. "The song is a prayer—once such an empty aspect of my life, but always a full rich part of hers. I don't know how but once again I feel the contradiction between deep sorrow, with streaks of unbelievable joy and gratitude. I don't understand. Now is not the time to figure it out. The word that keeps coming to me is 'grace'."

Friendship is always a grace, even when it is full of challenge, and that is why it remains a useful analogy for a mature relationship with God. Friendship with God, like human friendship, is a grace that is not precluded because human beings are so different from God. Despite apparent obstacles, what starts out as a one-sided companioning presence of God can flower into friendship and mutuality as the Book of Wisdom shows. The Book of Wisdom speaks of the personification of wisdom, Sophia, who "passes into holy souls and makes them friends of God and prophets." Those who are friends of God will not necessarily enjoy worldly success or amass riches; they will even be looked upon as foolish because of their loftier concerns. But they will discover the unsurpassable grace that comes from the evolution of their relationship with God into friendship.

As we come to appreciate fuller dimensions of the companion image of God, we may become ready to discover fuller dimensions of other images of the hidden God. Among them is the image of God as compassionate adversary, which the next chapter takes up.

9

God as Compassionate Adversary

Most of us are not inclined to think about adversaries as a positive part of our spiritual life. Conflict, especially with God, is a situation we feel we ought to avoid or get rid of quickly. Yet if we think about it more carefully, trying to understand apparent opposition presents an opportunity to address neglected dimensions of a relationship with God.

The image of God as adversary, like other images, is a metaphorical way of talking about a relationship. It is not to be taken literally. As with some other images of God, the term describes a quality of relationship at a given time, as opposed to describing the character of another. It is not a permanent condition and says more about our own response and behavior than it does about the nature or intentions of God.

When we suffer injustice or something happens to put us at odds with others, we instinctively treat those who offended us as "enemies." We do the same thing to God. When something dear to us is threatened and affects our spiritual life, we feel the urge to start relating to God as an adversary. The first evidence of this for most of us is a change in attitude toward God, either through distancing, resentment, or confrontation.

For many of us, the perception of God as hostile or uninterested moves us to distance ourselves emotionally. Without questioning our perception, and the ideas it is based on, we drift away from the God who formerly grounded us. While most of us would probably be reluctant to speak of God as an opponent, the way we perceive and react suggests that it is easy to fall into such an attitude without naming it as such.

It doesn't always take a major event to make us start distancing ourselves from God: disappointment, boredom, or self-sufficiency can be enough. We can feel a widening divide when God does not seem responsive or relevant to our concerns. The distance helps us to protect ourselves from the demands of relationship or to avoid questioning our own agendas. With distancing and self-protection it is easy not to notice how we create and maintain the perception of God as an adversary. Resentment, like distancing, often overtakes the spirit quietly without our being aware of it. A slowly smoldering resentment creates a smoke screen that clouds understanding. It takes perceptive self-knowledge to notice the beginnings of resentment, which may start as a feeling of righteous indignation. When God, who was thought to be a powerful ally, fails to provide the support we expected, we feel justified in regarding God as against us. Once this indignation takes root, resentment arises and, not long after, enmity. These attitudes are not easily dispelled.

A woman interviewed a year after losing her husband in a senseless act of violence said she could no longer pray. She argues that her prayer didn't protect her from tragedy or danger. Her resentment prevents her from even approaching God. Before she lost her husband, she might have reasoned that God doesn't cause tragedy. But when she was caught in its grip, raw emotion took over and colored her reasoning. She felt she had to do something with the intense emotional pain she felt. The faceless terrorist was far away. Who could she blame or resent but the one whom she had looked to as protector? God, she now reasoned, was responsible for failing to prevent the act of violence. She resentfully turned a cold shoulder to God.

Confrontation presents an alternative to turning a cold shoulder. A man who lost thirty friends in the attack on the World Trade Center says he confronts God by lashing out at God regularly. He curses God for letting such a tragedy happen.

This man claims he holds a remnant of his faith in a Trinitarian God. He says he can still accept Jesus the Son, but he has a huge problem with the all-powerful Father. The powerful Father, who should be able to do anything but fails to, no longer serves his faith. Ironically, this idea of the powerful but unfeeling God he rejects still has great power over him, but he does not question the adequacy of his idea of God's power.

Most of us assume that our understanding of power is adequate and transferable to God. But the power we attribute to God too easily mirrors the ideas of human power we have inherited, often beginning with the power represented by our parents. A parental image of God may be positive and reassuring, but it also has the ability to generate negative reactions. It reassures us when we have fear or seek comfort, but that same image has the potential to foster intense negative feeling, as when a parental God disappoints us or fails to rescue us from harm.

To understand the spiritual implications of an adversarial relationship and to balance a one-sided tendency to view it negatively, several conditions ought to be noted. Labeling someone as an adversary is based on perceptions (which can be poorly founded). Perceived opposition isn't necessarily a permanent condition. And the apparent negative quality of an adversary may hide positive aspects. To explore these conditions, we begin with the biblical tradition that recognizes that conflict has the potential to bring about a stronger and more richly textured faith, especially when someone discovers a hidden compassion in the other.

The Compassionate Adversary in the Hebrew Scriptures

We learn positive ways of dealing with adversaries from observing those who face them with courage and hope. The Hebrew Scriptures offer some vivid examples. Saul and David, the first kings of Israel, were intermittently friends and enemies. At one point David is hiding in a cave with his men while Saul pursues him. Saul enters the cave to relieve himself. Hiding in the dark innermost part of the cave, David is close enough to Saul to kill him easily. Instead, David stealthily cuts off a corner of his cloak. When Saul is a safe distance away from the cave, David calls after him as he holds up the corner of Saul's cloak.

David says to Saul, "Why do you listen to the words of those who say, 'David seeks to do you harm'? This very day your eyes have seen how the Lord gave you into my hand in the cave; and some urged me to kill you, but I spared you. I said, 'I will not raise my hand against my lord; for he is the Lord's anointed.'" When David is finished speaking, Saul responds that David is more righteous than he is because he has repaid evil with good. Saul says, "Who has ever found an enemy and sent the enemy safely away?" Who has, except for a compassionate adversary? Yet the paradox of a compassionate opponent is hard to grasp. Even the Bible often finds it easier to regard human beings either as one or the other.

The psalms are filled with references to adversaries. At times the psalmist complains about them, at times asks God to rise up in anger against their fury, and at times even relates to God as if God were an enemy. God feels like an adversary when feelings of abandonment, illness, or despair overtake the psalmist. When God seems to lack fairness or compassion over a period of time, even faithful or committed people can sometimes perceive God as against them.

Job regarded God as a kind of opponent who seemed to be the source of his suffering. Job had lost his health, his wealth, and most of his family. When his friends suggested his suffering was a punishment for his sin, Job disagreed. He knew he hasn't sinned but felt there had to be a reason for his suffering. He expected fairness from God, but when he finally questioned God, his questioning seemed to have no result. In the end, however, God turned out to be compassionate toward Job. God not only restored Job's fortunes, but God also taught Job that he must be compassionate toward those who dogmatically claimed to know God's "motives" or intentions.

While Job's interaction with God doesn't leave us with the impression that Job appreciates the value of confronting God as adversary, another biblical figure does. The book of Genesis describes an incident in which the patriarch Jacob wrestled with a stranger all through the night. The occasion reveals a great deal about the possibilities for growth that come from facing conflict.

Jacob had lived for many years in a land far from his homeland. When he decided to leave that land, he set out for an area where he knew he would meet his estranged twin brother, Esau, whom he had wronged years before. The night before Jacob was to meet Esau, Jacob stayed back alone without his family or servants. In the dark of the long night, he encountered an adversary who is sometimes described as an angel. They wrestled all night. When the man/angel did not prevail over Jacob, he struck Jacob's hip and put it out of joint.

The stranger was about to leave, but the wounded Jacob would not let him go until he gave him a blessing. The one with whom he contended tells him he will have a new name, Israel, because "you have striven with God and with humans and have prevailed." The "enemy" has helped Jacob discover who he is.

Jacob perceives the encounter as a wrestling with God. "I have seen God face to face, and yet my life is preserved, he says." After that, wounded yet blessed, he walks with a limp. Accepting his wounded condition makes it possible for him to face and accept his inner vulnerability.

Jacob was a complex individual who still lived under the shadow of his earlier deceitful ways. He had been shrewd and tenacious. He got his way no matter what he had to do even if it meant taking advantage of others. As he wrestles with God in the person of the angel-enemy, he also confronts the shadows within himself. We can only wonder what inner demons he faced in his struggle, what destructive tendencies and unresolved issues from the past plagued his conscience.

The incident of wrestling with the stranger takes place the night before Jacob was to meet and deal with the brother he feared might kill him and his family. He has already sent servants to placate Esau by presenting him with gifts, but he still does not know what to expect. The younger Jacob would have tried to outsmart his brother. The transformed, older Jacob, who had wrestled with God, was no longer concerned with protecting his ego. When Jacob finally meets Esau, he greets his brother with kindness and generosity. He offers him gifts, and, when Esau wants them to journey side by side, Jacob chooses a place behind. Limping from his wound, he lets his brother go on ahead while he keeps pace with the children and the cattle. His acceptance of vulnerability becomes the source of a new kind of strength. By relinquishing the need to prevail over his brother, Jacob experiences his compassion. And he makes peace with the enemies within himself—his competitiveness, his pride, and his self-sufficiency.

Jacob confronts an ineffable mystery when he wrestles with God. In the process, he discovers a truth about himself beyond words. He encounters God as the ultimate Other and, at the same time, as the source of his deepest self. Jacob learns that facing what he fears can lead to a truth that is personal and liberating, a truth that changes his perception of others. He learns to trust that there are some kinds of truth that can only be discovered by wrestling with God.

Compassion for Opponents in the Christian Scriptures

When the Christian Scriptures take up the theme of conflict with opponents, God rarely appears as adversary. If God appears as an opponent it is mostly when sinners, who are adversaries of God, make God an adversary. The New Testament focuses more on the attitude human beings ought to have toward those who oppose them. Jesus admonishes his followers to relate to enemies with love as God does.

In Matthew's Sermon on the Mount, Jesus proclaims love of enemies as a reversal of contemporary religious wisdom. He says, "You have heard that it was said, 'You shall love your neighbor and hate your enemy.' But I say to you, Love your enemies and pray for those who persecute you, so that you may be the children of your Father in heaven; for he makes his sun rise on the evil and on the good, and sends rain on the righteous and on the unrighteous."

His followers are invited not necessarily to like those who oppose them but to become compassionate toward them. They may, at some point, grow to like an adversary, but that is not essential. To become compassionate toward others it helps to enter into their experience, to realize that hostile behavior may not be that at all, and even when behavior is hostile it can be forgiven. Jesus exemplifies the ultimate attitude toward opponents: he forgives them freely and wishes them to be transformed into friends.

Besides teaching the love and forgiveness of adversaries, Jesus exemplifies it as he prays during the crucifixion, "Father, forgive them; for they do not know what they are doing." Is he giving his opponents the benefit of doubt, that in this instance they were not aware of the implications of their decision to put him to death? Or, is he suggesting even more? Do his words imply, much more than we can realize, that whenever we act out of hatred or revengeful anger, it is because we do not understand how we are obstructing the love of God that would flow through us?

Saint Paul, who persecuted the followers of Jesus, did not realize whom he was opposing when he lashed out against the first Christians. He thought he was defending God and opposing those who were God's enemies. Through a personal revelation of Christ he discovered that he himself was the adversary. He did not realize he was holding on to an *idea* of God instead of following where God was leading him.

At some times, for some people, it is necessary to confront the idea of God as an adversary in order to arrive at a fuller truth. Some people have to undergo a purgation of ideas (even good ideas) and a purgation of feelings (even legitimate feelings) by wrestling with God, who can loosen their prejudices. Wrestling with God is a symbolic way of saying that we can come to a new relationship with those who seem to oppose us by transforming our thoughts and healing our feelings.

Wrestling with God

The French philosopher Simone Weil observed, "One can never wrestle enough with God if one does so out of pure regard for the truth."[1] Weil, who died of starvation in 1943, did not doubt the existence of God. Nor did she speak of God as an adversary. Yet the way she wrestled with God shows she did not relate to God simply as an affable friend. By wrestling with God, she found a way to critique her ideas of God so she would not be worshipping an idea instead of God.

Weil struggled with what she regarded as partial, and therefore misleading, representations of God. She did not want to settle for a view of God that was based on doctrine defined by one particular religion. Though Weil regarded herself spiritually as a Christian, she did not embrace Christianity in its entirety. She says she never had "even for a moment, the feeling that God wants me to be in the church." Because her conception of life was Christian, she felt herself already spiritually in the Christian community. She saw no need, and in fact considered it intellectual dishonesty, to add dogma to her conception of life. She felt that remaining apart from the institutional church enabled her to continue wrestling with God.

Weil thought that this sort of wrestling with God kept her honest. It allowed her to see the difference between the living God and ideas of God, and freed her from requiring that God conform to her ideas. Weil's insistence on the importance of wrestling with God suggests that certain ideas can turn God into an opponent. Until we wrestle with God, we may not know how much more there is to God than the ideas we have come to regard as essential.

Though wrestling with God can sometimes appear to be an intellectual exercise, the impulse to struggle with God to arrive at truth arises from somewhere deeper in the psyche. To get at that place it may be useful to begin with the intellect to discover its limits. This wrestling is like the struggle of a Zen student who ponders a koan.

A Zen teacher gives a student an apparently insoluble question, such as what is the sound of one hand clapping. The student is told to ponder it and return with an answer. Since the koan does not have a logical answer, the student's challenge is to get beyond conventional or rational thinking in responding. The teacher looks for a breakthrough in the student's way of approaching a problem. If the student gets stuck in an old way of approaching questions, she or he remains captive to a limited way of thinking. The teacher knows the student is on the road to truth when the student's response comes from a genuine personal confrontation with the hidden nature of things.

What the student is struggling with in considering a koan is not the question it presents, but the mind or self that perceives. Likewise, when the mind perceives God as an adversary, what the believer is struggling with is not God simply as an opponent but the mind's reluctance to move past its one-dimensional view that others are either for us or against us. To wrestle with God is to begin to penetrate the deeper truth of relationship and to open oneself to the possibility of a larger vision.

Moving beyond Enmity

Wrestling with God involves not just ideas but also feelings. When feelings of conflict are allowed to rise to consciousness without fear or guilt, they can be therapeutic. Gerard Manley Hopkins, a nineteenth-century Jesuit poet, shows this when he speaks to God as an opponent who must be moved to compassion. In the sonnet "Thou Art Indeed Just," he voices his frustration with a God who seems not to hear him.[2]

Hopkins believes that God is just but reminds God that the poet is also concerned with justice. He asks why sinners prosper while he, who has dedicated his life to God, sees his efforts wither. Even plants and animals without intelligence flourish, while he does not. God does not seem to respond to his desire to give his life to God. He says he doesn't understand how he could fare worse if God were his enemy rather than his friend.

In the poem Hopkins does not break through to a rational resolution of his questions. An "answer" is not likely to cure his frustration. But in freely voicing his feelings, Hopkins allows them to carry him to his deepest yearning. At the end of the poem, he lets go of his lament, and he simply pleads with God, the center of his life, to "send my roots rain." His heart is ready to wait in trust for the right conditions for his feelings to be healed.

A character in Kathy Hepinstall's novel *The House of Gentle Men* offers insight into this slow movement toward reconciliation with an adversary. Charlotte, the main character, began treating God as an adversary after she conceived a child as the result of rape.[3] Unable to deal with the situation, she abandoned the child shortly after it was born. The child was found and survived not far from where Charlotte lived.

Charlotte says, long afterward, that she abandoned her newborn son because "I needed to be enemies with God. It helped harden my heart." By hardening her heart, she protected herself from the memory of rape and the fear of continuing vulnerability. She was able to deal with her feelings about God years later, after she came to know her attacker and after she saw how the boy had developed. She came to know both of them, not as a reminder of her painful past but as real persons who could move her heart.

She came to forgive the person who raped her as she saw him in pain over guilt for his act. She learned to love him. Charlotte says she realized that the God who disappeared from her sight had grown bigger. God returned as a loved one who could evoke compassion in her.

Any of us can feel ourselves as adversaries of God when we are growing through a painful transition. Reconciliation comes only when we can get beyond the hardened heart's way of feeling and the mind's peculiar way of reasoning about opponents. When the defenses are down, compassion can come in.

When defense is no longer the primary response in a situation of opposition, amazing reconciliations can occur. Stanley Weintraub tells a true story of such reconciliation and compassion between adversaries.[4] In December of 1914 enemies along the front lines in the First World War put aside their weapons to celebrate a holiday together. Their spontaneous gesture was not ordered or approved of by their leaders. Their strong desire to celebrate humanity's deepest hopes for peace, in a tradition common to both, overshadowed whatever concern they had for the approval of their superiors.

As the holiday approached, a cold rain muddied the fields and flooded trenches. Soldiers ate their rations in the midst of rodents, barbed wire, and filth, not to mention gunfire and death. By December 4, a lax attitude was developing between the opponents. The sides were not firing at mealtimes, and they occasionally threw newspapers weighted with stones to the other side. On December 16 some Germans, holding up their hands, left their trenches to take in the wounded. English forces followed suit. The Germans gestured to come over and when the English did, the Germans helped them bury the dead. They chatted, smoking one another's cigarettes.

The episode hinted of a more celebratory truce. A week before Christmas the Germans sent a luscious chocolate cake into the British line with an invitation to attend the captain's birthday party. It was accepted, and the Germans entertained with a series of songs. This was a precursor to the Christmas truce.

Even though the commanders urged the troops to be vigilant in case of attack during the holiday, the soldiers were not eager to fight at Christmas. Around six o'clock on Christmas Eve the scene grew strangely quiet. At eleven the men were exchanging visits between the trenches. Sometime during the night a Christmas tree appeared on the German side. And then, a rich baritone voice was heard singing, "Stille Nacht, Heilige Nacht." At one spot, five Germans shouted for someone to arrange a cease-fire for the day, to come out armed only with wine, sweets, and cigarettes. All along the front line, "enemies" approached one another with gifts and carols.

The cautious initiatives must have come from a deeply rooted desire because, despite occasional shootings and even a few deaths, the truce took hold. The men on the line did not want to fight, even though British commanders were concerned that the soldiers would lose their aggressive edge. The soldiers knew better than the commanders that "enemy" is a relative term.

These stories shed light on one of the things that make people become adversaries—the perception of a hostile agenda. Enemies are often presumed to be guided only by a desire to undermine the well-being of another. The idea carries over into perceptions of God. When we assume God to have an inscrutable will that opposes or is insensitive to our best interests, God becomes adversary.

Some of us are driven by a strong desire to figure God out. If we just knew why certain things happen, we think we could have faith and not slip into viewing God as adversary. We are convinced that mysterious or not, God ought to be able to make sense to us. Maybe we ought to stop thinking of God as having an agenda and instead open ourselves to the possibility that God's presence is more basic than that. A tremendous burden would be removed from our relationship with God. We would no longer approach conflict as a clash between two egos.

This chapter's reflection on God as Compassionate Adversary makes it evident that ego exerts a subtle influence on the way we approach God and ourselves. The next chapter, which addresses the image of God as Fertile Emptiness, seeks to unravel some of the influence of ego.

10

God as Fertile Emptiness

One of the paradoxes of Christian spirituality is that to appreciate the fullness of the mystery of God, it is necessary to enter into emptiness. The meaning of emptiness, however, is not immediately apparent even aside from its being part of this paradox. To appreciate its meaning and importance, we need to take a closer look at the notion of emptiness, at our own emptiness, and at the relation of emptiness to the fullness underneath all that we say about God.

The idea of emptiness has both negative and positive connotations. Webster's Encyclopedic Dictionary defines emptiness as "containing nothing; void of the usual or appropriate contents." According to this definition, the negative aspect, "containing nothing," implies an identifiable form to start with, such as an empty house or an empty container. The form is devoid of what we expect. On the positive side, the notion of emptiness suggests possibility and the capacity to be filled.

When we are considering emptiness in a spiritual sense, we need to expand its meaning further. Spiritually, emptiness does not refer merely to something that is missing, like a glass that has nothing in it. If we think of emptiness this way, then things have meaning only if they take up space and displace something else. Spiritual emptiness refers to the human capacity for God, openness to respond to the presence of God as it manifests itself. Spiritual emptiness allows the divine and human to coexist, while it puts the affairs of life into perspective.

The language of emptiness is the language of metaphor. It is not to be taken literally. In comparing what we know in one area to what is more difficult to grasp in another area, metaphorical language allows us to get at dimensions of experience that are not accessible by ordinary means. Whether we say we are "running on empty" when we have no reserve of energy or we say we have "emptied ourselves of false hopes," this language captures a complex experience more successfully than direct language does.

As these brief observations suggest, the notion of emptiness should be approached with the heart as well as the mind. Emptiness of heart implies the dissolution of emotional barriers to God such as resentment or fear. Emptiness of mind points to the dismantling of intellectual obstacles to trust in God. By probing emptiness of heart and mind, we can discover room to encounter God. We can also get a better sense of what gets in the way of a more intimate relationship with the fullness of the self-emptying God.

Human Emptiness before God

Living in an affluent society promotes the accumulation of surplus, from excess clothing to redundant paperwork. While an itch to organize and reduce physical clutter may reduce the excess periodically, spiritual baggage is not so easily dispensed with. An abundance of words and concepts about God and religion can seem as essential as the stored mementos that preserve our history; we can be just as reluctant to let go of them.

Mental clutter gets in the way of openness to God. A story from the Buddhist tradition illustrates the problem. A Japanese master, Nan-in, once received a university professor who wanted to inquire about Zen.[1] The master served the visitor a cup of tea. As he kept pouring the tea even after the cup was full, the professor objected, saying it could hold no more. Nan-in then told him that he was like the cup, full of opinions and speculations. There was no room to hear the message of Zen. So it is with us.

If we are full of ourselves and our ideas, we have trouble seeing things in a larger perspective. It is difficult to listen patiently to the silent speech of God that makes emptiness meaningful. Emptiness reveals fullness: it is the open door to the true self and the hidden

God. That door is often closed as we go through the ego-work of daily survival. Our incessantly active minds keep sorting out what is useful or useless, desirable or undesirable, what is mine or not mine, what is God or not God. All these distinctions close off access to the emptiness that reveals the presence of God. When we allow the door to the true self to open, our frantic activity is put into perspective. The true self is revealed as the inexhaustible ground beneath our overactive minds.

There are many things in our minds that get in the way of such an openness and emptiness. Our minds, like our lives, are crowded with all sorts of notions and feelings. Some are helpful for achieving goals, and some are part of working out relationships. Some are simply random associations. What goes on incessantly in this variety of areas often barely rises to the level of consciousness. "Voices" from beneath awareness keep murmuring while we think we are giving full attention to the task at hand.

One can't help wondering if the mind's busyness might be related to a fear of emptiness. When we turn to God in thought, prayer, or intention, we soon find ourselves turning back to more practical matters. We want to wiggle out of confronting an emptiness that makes us uncomfortable. It seems so hard to leave ourselves open to the silence that allows us to listen to God. Our natural tendency is to look for something definite to hang on to—a familiar idea, a comforting image, a word someone else has taught us, someone else's prayer. These may not always feel like our own, but we are not accustomed to waiting for emptiness to reveal what is our own. Because emptiness sounds negative, even frightening, we shun the thought of it. Yet it holds a key to meeting the hidden God. The beatitudes show us this.

In Matthew's Gospel the first beatitude states, "Blessed are the poor in spirit; the kingdom of heaven is theirs." The poor who are blessed are the empty, those who come with begging bowls, ready to receive what God gives at the moment. They do not dwell on what they do not have or what is superficial. They leave ample room for God to enter their hearts. The beatitude is a reminder of the need to be empty before God in order to hear the silent word God speaks.

Silence is a cousin of emptiness. In her essay "A Field of Silence" Annie Dillard describes how she discovered this.[2] She was walking through a farm near where she lived, observing some roosters when she was suddenly overwhelmed by a sense of silence. The sounds around her seemed to stop, as if nature were holding its breath, while silence gripped her. A profound silence revealed to her the real world, the "God-blasted, paralyzed day."

Dillard's momentary experience of the deep silence that suffused everything left its mark. She felt as if God had spoken and said, "I am here, but not as you have known me. This is the look of silence. . . ." The encounter was so monumental that she couldn't dwell on it any further right then, but it burrowed its way into her psyche and left her with the conviction that spirits inhabited that empty field, and every other space.

Dillard's account of her experience of God's presence was not based on a fixed idea of God, not on the direct awareness of a being that fit her concept of the divine. Dillard felt the divine, not as something she knew, but as a presence that knew her. This presence was and remains hidden.

The hidden presence of God symbolized by emptiness also resonates for the poet Rumi, who speaks of emptiness as an insistent human longing for God. Rumi wrote of the emptiness of the reed through which the soul makes music in the world. Without the open reed, and the holes in the reed, there could be no sound. Yet within the notes are secrets few will hear. If the reed could speak for itself, Rumi says, it would pour out its lament at being separated from the reed bed, its homesickness for God; yet it learns to wait, content to be hollow.

A noted commentator on the work of Rumi, Coleman Barks, says that Rumi has a whole theory of language based on the reed flute.[3] Barks says that Rumi suggests that beneath everything we say, in each note, lies a nostalgia for the reed bed. Language and music arise because of the hollowness of the reed and its longing for home. Language is not important in itself, but only in its ability to give voice to what emanates from the center. The human center is rooted in God, the Hidden Center.

The Emptiness of God

When we speak of God, most of us give the impression that we know what the word *God* means. We associate it with certain qualities, such as infinite goodness, power, and justice, as well as with images that represent them. These qualities are limited by the meaning we give them, but rarely do we stop to consider those limits. The power we attribute to God is power as we define it; goodness is fairness as we assess it. Because language and the thought that generates it are limited, it takes an emptying of concepts to move us toward the reality of God.

Mystics and apophatic theologians know that concepts of God are not the same as God. The mystic Meister Eckhart indicated the difference by using the lowercase *god* when he wanted to identify a human conception of God and the uppercase *God* when he wanted to call attention to the unconditioned reality beyond human concepts.[4] Eckhart says that one does not penetrate to the Godhead itself by ideas and images until one is willing to acknowledge human emptiness:

> The intellect that peers into and penetrates all the corners of the Godhead . . . is not content with goodness, nor with wisdom, nor the truth, no, nor even with God himself. To tell the truth, it is no more content with (the idea of) God than it would be with a stone or a tree. It can never rest until it gets to the core of the matter, crashing through to that which is beyond the idea of God and truth, until it reaches the *in principio*, the beginning of beginnings, the origin or source of all goodness and truth.[5]

As the source of being, God cannot be objectified. God cannot be contained in an expression that allows us to hold on to the meaning of God. This is why God is spoken of not just as Emptiness, but as Fertile Emptiness, overflowing and full of possibility.

For Christians, emptiness finds expression in the person and life of Jesus. In his Letter to the Philippians, Saint Paul speaks of Jesus "emptying" himself of godly superiority and taking the form of a slave with no personal or spiritual possessions to claim as his own. Paul uses the idea of Jesus' self-emptying not only to reveal the transparency of Jesus to God but also to admonish his listeners to model their behavior on the behavior of Jesus.

The claim that Jesus embodies God's self-emptying is, at the same time, a claim about human self-emptiness. The ego, our conscious awareness of the self, is taken to be the highest expression of what it means to be human. It allows us to know ourselves and to take responsibility for our actions. But it can also create illusions and isolate us from one another and from God. To transcend these limiting aspects of ego by "emptying" or forgetting is to come into contact with the larger self we seek in God.

By transcending the limits of the human ego, Jesus reveals how human beings can live in freedom out of the center of a true self. He also reveals something about the emptiness of God, namely that the self-emptying God who dwells within human beings is not driven by divine ego concerns. It is surprising how much of what we say of God seems to imply a divine or ultimate ego.

Expressions like the will of God and the honor of God create the impression that God operates out of a psychological ego center like our own. We can try to interpret these less egocentrically, but Jesus does that for us by his words and examples. The teaching and behavior of Jesus reflect an attitude that is forgetful of ego. His attitude ought to make us more critical of the way we apply the language of ego to God. We get help applying his attitude from a rediscovery of the apophatic tradition, which is making itself felt again today.

Apophatic Tradition Today

The word *apophatic* comes from the Greek word *apophasis*, which means to deny something while at the same time referring to it ("I will not mention her many virtues"). It aims to speak of God while also saying it is impossible to speak directly about God. The apophatic tradition has a long history in Christian theology and spirituality, yet it has always been a minor theme compared to the preference for a more positive approach.

The apophatic approach is not something many people can easily comprehend or rest in, but some people are growing more comfortable with it as they come to realize the limits of language. Apophatic theology can't avoid language, or even images like darkness or clouds, but by pointing out the limits of language it helps people today not to put absolute trust in concepts.

The apophatic approach is gaining interest today, perhaps in part because certain beliefs have become problematic even for people who still maintain a basic faith. In particular, when persons who have been faithfully seeking God for a long time find themselves in situations in which their customary ideas about God no longer adequately fit their experience, it is likely they will look for another way to express their faith. They may find themselves moving toward a more apophatic approach.

Doris Grumbach traces her journey toward an apophatic spirituality in a book that recounts a major shift in her spiritual life. Grumbach begins her book by recalling a powerful experience of God she had many years earlier.[6] Grumbach was sitting alone on the steps outside a small house in Millwood, New York, when she felt herself overwhelmed with a sense of God's presence. It penetrated her thoroughly, and she pondered what it could mean for someone who previously had no interest in God.

She slowly nurtured her new interest in God. She began to go to church and developed a spiritual life that sustained her for fifty years. But late in life, after much reflection, she became convinced that she had to turn to a different kind of prayer, a more contemplative prayer that would take her away from communal ritual into a strange new territory. In this spiritual territory the absence of God would turn out to be as important as the presence of God.

In the beginning of *The Presence of Absence*, Grumbach quotes the writer Paul Valéry speaking about the beauty of the empty page, the setting from which miracles will emerge. He says that the presence of absence reflects the absolute in all beauty that forbids our touching it. It sends forth something sacred, striking with doubt and awe the one who is about to act. This is the theme of Grumbach's present experience of God—fullness in emptiness.

In the course of the several years of prayer that the book chronicles, Grumbach grapples with emptiness and the act of emptying. Her memoir is a record of her search rather than a description of a method of contemplation. As she reads extensively on the experience of absence, she begins to appreciate the kind of emptiness that can contribute to growth in the practice of contemplative prayer.

Grumbach reads that "Absence takes precedence over presence, or better said, is the first form of presence." If this is the case, she muses, then the cloud of her unknowing may one day contain God's presence. "The emptiness of my present prayer, perhaps, may shape His appearance if the sense of God should ever arrive. And what is best of all, the seed planted in me on the Millwood steps might sprout into a prescribed shape, a Presence determined by long absence."

Grumbach recounts a journey many religious people would find to be a frightening negation. It would seem that God as Companion, especially a companion like Jesus, would present a more desirable image than Emptiness. But we cannot choose our images of God at will; they arise from experience. When darkness and impasse present themselves and overshadow other images, there often appears to be no choice but to surrender to the challenge of the moment. Grumbach tried to do that.

Grumbach's experience, personal as it is, is not totally unique. Others in our age have recounted similar situations where the absence or emptiness of God impressed them more powerfully than the familiar positive sense of presence they formerly felt. This perception of God reflects a cultural climate that is also taken up with the meaning hidden in what appears to be empty.

Poetic Imagination and the Inexpressible

In 2004 the Institute of Contemporary Art in Philadelphia organized a city-wide initiative called *The Big Nothing*. It included programs at more than thirty-five museums, science centers, and performing arts venues. The project explored a topic that has intrigued artists and scientists, especially in the twentieth century, but the project's promotional literature recognizes that *nothing* or *emptiness* has been a recurring subject throughout history.

The topic of nothingness has had spiritual relevance in a number of religious traditions from the biblical presentation of creation out of nothing to Buddhism's ancient notion of *sunyata* or emptiness. Though other aspects of the Hebrew and Christian traditions have received more attention, now it is time to give attention to this less directly felt and less articulated dimension of the spiritual life.

Undoubtedly many contemporary factors contribute to this interest in the void. The shift from a world of solid substances to a world of relations and change may be just one such factor. A new awareness of the limits of language may be another. Whatever the reasons for the emerging interest in emptiness, the phenomenon offers an opportunity to get a fresh perspective on relating to God.

The Image of God as Fertile Emptiness allows for a different way of seeing things. Direct vision isn't the only way to approach a topic. If it were, we could never sense a car speeding at us from the side before we see it or a great idea lurking at the edges of consciousness. Like the knowledge we have of something moving at the edge of our field of vision, we can sense a divine presence through a kind of spiritual peripheral vision. This is an intuitive knowledge that is not easily expressed in specific images or words.

Peripheral vision offers one analogy for intuiting the mystery of God. Negative space offers another. In recent years, increasing attention has been given to negative space in art. Negative space is the space at the edges, around, and between the main objects in a painting. It refers to the relative emptiness in a work of art which we do not usually think of as important to the content.

The vast empty space of the practice room in Degas's painting of ballet class, the opening within a bent elbow in his sculpture of a young dancer—these are examples of negative space. The space is not literally empty; it only appears so because the eye is focused elsewhere. When the eye is focused on one spot, we need to be reminded that the negative space that surrounds the object is just as important for its particular character. Negative space reminds us that we can be so busy looking for the God we think we know that we miss the God we have not yet come to recognize.

All this talk about emptiness should remind us that despite centuries of words and images for God, God is still a bottomless well that the human mind cannot fathom. We grope for a way to talk about God, even to think about God, but the breadth and depth of God elude us. Poets, who depend on words, understand better than anyone the power and limits of language.

The twentieth-century poet T. S. Eliot uses language to point to the fertile emptiness of God. He threads the insights of the mystics through *The Four Quartets* to demonstrate that emptiness reveals what words cannot, a fullness beyond imagination.

In *The Four Quartets* Eliot sets out to explore the question of how we can live in time so as to conquer time.[7] Eliot reflects on the question by putting himself in four places—Burnt Norton, East Coker, the Dry Salvages, and Little Gidding. As he moves through each of these, the search for liberation from sin takes him on a journey toward love. The "answer" he discovers reflects the paradoxes of emptiness. His poetic journey leads to an emptiness illuminated by the mystics.

John of the Cross was one of the mystics Eliot drew on directly. Borrowing John's insights, Eliot observes that to arrive where you are, to find joy in your own destiny, you have to go by a way without ecstasy, without knowledge, and without possessions. The only thing you will know is what you don't know. Emptiness is the way.

One of his interpreters, Lyndall Gordon, writes that Eliot set out to be a vacuum for grace to fill, learning to surrender to it without relying on the usual spiritual works and notions of success, including spiritual success.[8] To advance toward this goal, Eliot relies on emptiness and absence, urging his soul to be still and to welcome the darkness because it is the darkness of God. He uses words to undermine words and ideas ("wait without thought") and to unite his own emptiness with the fullness of God.

Eliot and others use language to affirm and negate simultaneously. In this part on the paradoxical images of Challenging Companion, Compassionate Adversary, and Fertile Emptiness, I have tried to use images in the same way. Words break under the burden of God's truth. Let them break. Only then will we know that God cannot be contained in words.

Paradoxical language is intended to jolt us out of complacency. It reminds us that God is utterly transcendent as well as immanent, as people of deep faith have always known. But it also serves as an antidote for the glut of words and images that bombard us today. Traditional images can still serve us well, but they are so familiar we take them for granted. Only a purification of language through silence, or a bending and stretching of language, can reorient us to better understand the value and the limits of our traditional images for God.

With the purification of our thought and language for God comes a new challenge. Our current challenge in the journey with God is to learn what spiritual skills need to be cultivated to help us make our way through a world that is constantly changing. While some of the traditional skills can still serve us well, the world we live in presents situations that call for new responses. Part 3 examines what some of those skills are and how they might be cultivated.

III

Cultivating Spiritual Skills

11

New Challenges, New Spiritual Skills

In the last several chapters we considered several images of a God who journeys with us into new places. There we are challenged to develop spiritual skills that enable us to live anew with a hidden God. We might wonder why we don't just rely on the old spiritual skills. They are still useful.

The ability to express compassion for others, to control anger, to be generous—these are all as important as they ever were. But conditions in a new context call for a different use of skills. For example, even a virtue as simple as generosity can require a new kind of sensitivity and discernment in our complex world.

After the terrorist attack of September 11, 2001, Julie Salamon began to reflect on the various ways that concerned people responded generously to the families of victims, to workers at the scene, and to others who were involved.[1] Her reflection led her to explore the ways that generosity is expressed in our complex social world. The meaning of generosity seems self-evident; discerning how to express it isn't always obvious.

When people are moved to generosity today, they sometimes have to consider issues like tax deductions for charity, social services that are already responding to needs, the kinds of policies foundations ought to establish to maximize the effects of giving, and the value of non-monetary forms of giving. These issues couldn't be anticipated in an earlier age. They require people to be discerning in the way they express generosity. Salamon is aware of these issues and how they impinge on her own instinct to give, but she felt she needed to discern the nuances involved in applying generosity. For help in that she turned to the Jewish philosopher Maimonides and his *Ladder of Generosity*.

Maimonides wrote *Ladder of Generosity* in the thirteenth century. He uses the ladder as a framework to treat eight degrees of almsgiving from grudging giving to giving in order to empower. Salamon finds Maimonides' deceptively simple analogy opens a new avenue for understanding the many dimensions of this virtue for her, but she must adapt it as she applies it to situations in the twenty-first century.

We find ourselves facing a similar situation as we try to understand our relationship to a hidden God in today's world. We have the insights of Scripture and theology in the Christian tradition, but we need to discern how to apply the insights in our cultural situation. As a preamble to examining spiritual skills in several areas, it will be useful to consider some challenges in the contemporary spiritual landscape and what they have to tell us about the development of spiritual skills

Understanding the Contemporary Spiritual Landscape

Our spiritual forebears didn't have to deal with radical change as we do. Change was part of their lives, but it didn't have the impact on their religion that contemporary change has on ours. Religions other than their own were merely idolatry; they never appeared as genuine paths to God. Science as we know it didn't exist, so they didn't have to reexamine their assumptions about religion and God in the face of scientific explanations. Popular psychology didn't urge them to settle for emotional growth and to forget spiritual growth. Above all, they didn't find themselves answering one objection to their faith only to turn around and find themselves confronting new questions.

These and other conditions influence the culture in which we try to hold on to faith in a hidden and mysterious God. We can't take on all the challenges, but we can look at several areas that affect religion and spirituality. The areas of culture that I want to consider here are pluralism, information/technology, and self-knowledge. Because they challenge traditional expressions of faith in new ways, they call for the development of new spiritual skills.

The first of these situations is the pluralistic world we live in. When I was growing up in the years before the Second Vatican Council, the only religious diversity I knew was the difference between Catholics and Protestants (and I didn't know that very well). When I studied undergraduate theology, my attention was directed toward understanding my own tradition better. Doing graduate work, I began to read religious thinkers who were not Catholic, and slowly my perspective began to expand. As I came to know people whose relationship with God was rooted in other religious traditions, the God I related to earlier became too small.

Many of us grew up within a particular religious sub-culture that provided for all our spiritual needs. There was no need to know how other people related to God or what they thought. But now we find ourselves thrust into a world where there are many possibilities for thinking about God. Once we are exposed to the riches of a tradition other than our own, questions begin to arise. Few of us are prepared for the pluralistic world that presents us with diverse beliefs and practices. We often feel we lack the spiritual skills for dealing with pluralism in a spirit of faith.

We may begin to suspect God's boundless truth is hidden in a multitude of traditions. The God who will not be contained in a particular religion becomes more mysterious. Can we learn to live with that newfound mystery while remaining rooted in the tradition that has nourished us? Or must we choose our old religion, a new religion, or no religion at all?

Some have found ways to remain rooted in the religious tradition that nurtured them while opening up to insights into a hidden God from other religious perspectives. There is something to be learned from listening to other religious views. Then one realizes that each tradition has its strengths, as well as its weaknesses. For example, one excels in defending justice, another in revering the sacredness of the physical, and yet another in celebrating rituals. Those who have opened themselves to new sources of truth, without relinquishing their heritage, have had to learn to cultivate new spiritual skills as they expand their vision of God's presence in the world. They can help us with our skills.

The second of the cultural situations that calls for the cultivation of new skills is our immersion in a culture where knowledge is defined in informational units that are multiplied daily. We are bombarded with these chunks of data that make us feel we know what is going on. The flow of information is so constant that we turn to technology to manage it. Technology helps us multi-task so we can watch a conversation on television while a different message is scrolling across the bottom of the screen. Our understanding becomes fragmented. There seems to be no way to turn off the process to ask what is really important. Small wonder that we are dulled to the transcendent hidden in the simple and the ordinary.

An antidote to the fragmentation of understanding is a contemplative attitude, but the culture we live in discourages a contemplative attitude. It prevents us from being present to anything in a wholehearted way. Henry David Thoreau minded the effects of distractions, though present to a much lesser degree in his nineteenth-century world. Thoreau withdrew to Walden Pond for a period of time so that he could reclaim his soul in solitude and thoughtfulness. In his diaries he reflects on the conditions that are needed to come to a true understanding of the world he inhabits and his purpose in it.

Thoreau mused that it takes leisure to appreciate a single phenomenon. To Thoreau, appreciating a single phenomenon is akin to appreciating the world. "Unless the humming of a gnat is as the music of the spheres, and the music of the spheres is as the humming of a gnat, they are naught to me."[2] A sense of the importance of each experience, no matter how insignificant it appears, impels someone to give herself or himself wholly to it.

Personal presence represents the basis for a contemplative attitude that opens one to the hidden God. But neither popular culture nor popular religion has devoted much attention to the development of a contemplative attitude. And the informational and technological climate reinforces that resistance. The skills of a contemplative attitude are among those we need to learn by listening to those who are developing them in the midst of a busy culture.

The third situation that calls for new spiritual skills is the way our culture tends to view knowledge and self-knowledge. Knowledge is seen largely as information or as the practical ability to achieve certain results. Knowledge is used to attain practical goals that have immediate results. This doesn't leave much room for self-knowledge, which is part of a slow process of transformation. It doesn't leave much room to appreciate the irreducible mystery of who we are.

Despite the information explosion and the proliferation of ways to communicate, we have not made great strides in self-knowledge. There is little evidence in popular culture that individuals have come to greater understanding of why they hope, how they remember, how they can deal positively with emotions like anger and fear, and what resources they possess to cultivate their capacity for compassion or forgiveness. Self-knowledge takes more than information; it takes wisdom to discern how to live the mystery of being a creature who is both powerful and flawed.

To face the mystery of ourselves we need skills of self-knowledge that enable us to get beyond the superficial aspects of ourselves. Many of us think we know ourselves well because we know our opinions, our temperament, and our motivations. These are works of the ego. Genuine self-knowledge moves us beyond the habits of ego-thinking to a truer self.

Our culture, and our own self-protective instincts, can get in the way of meeting the true self. Self-help books, tapes, videos, and workshops promise to impart the spiritual self-knowledge we are looking for. Many of them promise a quick fix rather than genuine insight and slow transformation. We do not know how to come to a deeper understanding of ourselves, or we are afraid to find out.

In order to really come to know ourselves, we need to penetrate the illusions we have about ourselves, the trappings of knowledge that focus us on the ego self. Beneath that ego self lies a larger self. We come to know this larger self by cultivating spiritual skills of genuine self-knowledge, by learning from those who have taken this on in spite of living in a culture that largely fails to grasp the wisdom of self-knowledge.

Cultivating Spiritual Skills

Spiritual skills are related to virtues. While virtues are qualities of moral or religious strength, skills are the abilities that aid in developing and expressing virtue. From the earliest days of Christianity, faith, hope, and love stood out as the pre-eminent virtues. Not far behind were prudence, justice, temperance, and fortitude—the cardinal virtues. Along with these fundamental virtues, there were many others: humility, patience, wisdom, generosity, and so on. These subsidiary virtues supported the fundamental ones. Together they represent all the qualities one would expect in a person rooted in God, qualities that are still important.

Virtues are also understood as good habits that enable people to act according to their highest nature. Speaking of virtues as habits recognizes that they are dynamic and can develop. It also suggests that in certain situations or at certain times, different virtues are called for. One situation will require a person to put their habit of patience into practice while another will demand action and courage.

Spiritual skills help a person to discern what is needed in a particular time or situation. The relation between the two words, skill and spiritual, is important. A skill is "the ability, coming from one's knowledge, practice, aptitude, etc., to do something well." The spiritual is that which relates to the perception of meaning and order in the universe. It also relates to the way human beings understand themselves and their capacity to transcend their ego. Spiritual skills enable us to use our knowledge, religious and other, well in daily life. These skills enable us to integrate our beliefs and actions.

Cultivating spiritual skills means that a person learns to discern and practice faith in the midst of conflicting views of faith, to pray and live in a world that is fragmented and constantly changing, to know who he or she is in order to live authentically out of a true center. The way to cultivate the skills related to these areas cannot be laid out in advance. They grow as we learn from others and open ourselves to the God hidden in the midst of the world. In a global environment that means learning to live more freely, more deeply, and more expansively than before.

Spiritual Skills for an Expanding Universe

The spiritual landscape we have been reflecting on is large and diverse. Perhaps it is too large for most of us to ponder. We don't have to try to ponder all its detail of change, chaos, fragmentation, and teeming possibilities. We need only to open ourselves to the insight that we live in an organic world whose hidden movements toward order often elude us. We need only to be willing to cultivate more flexible spiritual skills that allow us to be at home in this environment. For many of us that calls for a shift of focus.

To find a focus that will accommodate a God who is larger than we ever imagined, virtues and their spiritual skills that command our attention need to be larger too. The importance of larger virtues is a theme that has been developed effectively by Natalia Ginzburg. Ginzburg says we should not promote the little virtues but great ones—not thrift but generosity, not caution but courage, not a desire for success but a desire to be and to know.[3] She says we usually do the opposite. Starting with the way we teach children, we emphasize the little virtues and hope the great virtues will spontaneously appear one day.

Ginzburg says we seem to think the great virtues are part of our instinctive nature, while the little ones appear to be the result of our efforts. Both arise from our deepest instincts, she says, but the little virtues tend to arise from a defensive instinct. We learn thrift more to avoid being in need than to benefit others. We learn tact more to avoid being judged rude than to tell the truth in love. With the little virtues, reason leads the way, and self-preservation is the goal.

The great virtues—courage, generosity, love of truth, love of neighbor—rise up from an instinct that does not rely on reason and which is difficult to name. They are more difficult to inculcate, but they will serve us better in developing a spiritual life suited to the age we live in. They will also rely on the help of more flexible and discerning spiritual skills, skills that are not calculated to produce immediate rewards.

Ginzburg warns that we should be cautious about promising and providing rewards for the cultivation of virtues. We mislead children when we teach them that their good behavior will benefit them in measurable ways. Rewards and punishments teach children to expect what life does not give. Good often goes unrewarded and evil goes unpunished. We will all suffer injustice.

If we teach children that virtue will be rewarded, they will assume that if they practice virtue they will be successful, have better relations with others, attain a better spiritual status, or earn God's favor. This attitude sets people up for disappointment; it obscures the truth that life's greatest gifts are hidden. Ginzburg suggests that if we want to foster an attitude of loving good and resisting evil, it will take more than a logical quid pro quo.

It takes a sense of vocation, she says, a passion for something worthwhile in itself and not personal gain, to nurture the great virtues. The kind of vocation she is talking about is a call and commitment to love because it is meaningful in itself apart from an external reward. We cannot impart a sense of vocation to others, but can only create a climate of space and silence that allows it to emerge. So also we cannot discover the true self or the God who eludes us unless we cultivate spiritual skills that create a climate of trust in what is hidden, reverence for God in the ordinary, and wisdom to accept dimensions of the self deeper than the ego.

Taking my cue from Natalia Ginzburg, I believe that the spiritual skills we seek in this age of a hidden God and a scattered self are skills that enlarge our hearts and minds while deepening our roots. The religious uncertainty that surrounds us should not drive us back to the small virtues that protect our security. Instead, we need to look to larger virtues and more freeing spiritual skills that relate to a more expansive God in a more expansive global environment.

The spiritual skills that respond most directly to the situation around us are the skills that enable us to live in the mystery of God and the mystery of ourselves, trusting that God will be with us as we make our mistakes and learn to find our way. Rather than helping us to stay the course that we already know, these spiritual skills will help us to launch out into unknown waters.

The spiritual skills that will help us most in this time of uncertainty will be skills that are discovered rather than known in advance. They will build on familiar classic virtues, but they will break new ground by giving us the proficiency to make our way through situations that call for courage, risk-taking, and new ways of seeing. In short, they are skills that will help us relate not only to a dynamic changing world but also to a God who will not be confined in our limited ideas and expectations.

The following chapters allow an opportunity to examine new spiritual skills in several areas. There are many more spiritual skills than those I have identified, but we need to start somewhere. I have chosen to start with skills relevant for our spiritual landscape with its diverse religious cultures, its obsession with information, its focus on narrow self-knowledge. To explore these areas the next few chapters will consider skills related to faith, contemplation, and the wisdom of self-knowledge, all with the goal of coming to a greater acceptance of a hidden God.

12

Cultivating Skills of Radical Faith

Among the most basic spiritual skills needed today are skills related to radical faith. Radical faith isn't the kind of faith that insists on adherence to all the doctrines of the church or the kind of faith that requires a literal interpretation of Scriptures. Radical faith is a faith rooted in God as its source and goal. It calls for a set of skills that foster the deep truth that God is greater than any limited set of beliefs or institutional affiliation, that God alone is the ground of life and hope.

Radical faith flows from a trusting relationship with a hidden God. What makes this faith radical and vital in the culture we inhabit is its ability to prioritize what is essential and what is secondary. God is essential, no matter how hidden, how mysterious, or how incomprehensible. Secondary are the means used to speak of God and to symbolize the relationship. In a complex, organic, changing, and fragmented world like ours it takes great determination to remain focused on God.

Contemporary culture does not have much patience with what is hidden. It doesn't offer much incentive to remain courageously focused on priorities. But patience and courage, those traditional virtues of the God-seeker, are only the first resources for radical faith. Besides these, there are more culture-specific skills whose shape we can't always recognize until we are in the midst of a situation that requires them.

Though we have to be in the midst of a situation to know the skills we lack, we can learn what some of them might be by listening to the experience of others. As we see others cope with new challenges to faith, we are able to identify some useful skills—the ability to live with multiple truths, to accept the mystery of God, to live confidently in the midst of ambiguity, and to act freely without being obsessed with results.

The Ability to Live with Multiple Truths

Religious diversity confronts us with a challenge relatively unknown to previous generations. Our spiritual ancestors lived, worked, and worshipped in a close community, an enclave of faith. Rarely were they exposed to religious possibilities outside their own faith community. We, however, live in a pluralistic environment. We mingle and converse with people in other denominations of our own tradition and even with those of different religious traditions. We may even find ourselves integrating the insights and practices of other traditions into our personal belief systems.

Diversity within the Christian tradition exposes some Christians to a broader range of ideas and experiences than those that originally nurtured them. When they can see value in divergent Christian perspectives, they may find themselves comfortably standing in two different places. Kathleen Norris is committed to a small Methodist church in South Dakota while she maintains a close relationship with the Benedictine monks at St. John's Abbey.[1] She attends her own local church and yet spends time in prayer at the abbey. The success of her book *Dakota: A Spiritual Geography* suggests that her readers understand her desire to embrace the best in both traditions.

Some have not confined their dialogue to groups within the Christian tradition but have found ways to marry insights from Eastern and Western religions. Fenton Johnson's participation in Buddhist meditation coupled with his prayer with the monks at Gethsemani helped him to work through his skepticism and to turn back to the Catholic faith he had rejected.[2] Johnson, like Norris, did not feel he had to reject one religious tradition in order to benefit from the other.

These attitudes represent a departure from the religious outlook that must seal itself off from other traditions in order to maintain its focus and identity. Some may, for various reasons, rightly find their religious convictions are at risk unless they maintain a clear separation between their beliefs or practices and the beliefs and practices of other religious traditions. Others, such as Norris and Johnson, have found that pluralism does not undermine their faith. Instead, it has made it possible for them to come to a new appreciation of their roots in a basic religious tradition and faith community. Interreligious dialogue has helped them find a God greater than any single view hidden in their own tradition.

Religious pluralism can present some problems and hazards, but it can also open some doors. One hazard is that exposure to a variety of religious perspectives can encourage people to nibble at a buffet of acceptable beliefs without encouraging them to mature commitment. But pluralism can also lead to a deeper appreciation of the infinite God who nourishes people through a variety of traditions. It can afford the seeker an opportunity to discover an unimaginably rich God present as mystery in a multitude of guises.

The Ability to Accept the Mystery of God

Exposure to a tradition other than one's own can lead to a wider perspective on the mystery of God. This happened to Diana Eck, director of the pluralism project at Harvard and a lifelong Methodist.[3] Eck grew up in Bozeman, Montana, where the only religion she knew was Christianity. It was a vital part of her life there. As Eck moved physically and spiritually from Montana to Massachusetts to India, however, she slowly discovered that her religious commitment to Christianity did not preclude her learning from other traditions. What she learned helped her to reinterpret her Christian faith and to enlarge her view of God.

When Eck's college interests led her to study in India for a year, she set out to learn all she could about Hinduism. Eck thought she would gain a new store of knowledge by investigating Hindu ideas of gods and goddesses. What she discovered was transformative. She was changed by immersing herself in the wisdom of a tradition different from her own.

Eck developed a friendship with a Hindu who made her realize that holiness can be found anywhere, not just among Christians. She surprised herself when she did not conclude that he ought to be a Christian. She also took to heart the noted Indian spiritual leader Krishnamurti's challenge to religious seekers that they not rely on concepts or judgments to hold on to religious values but that they find their own way to the spiritual. He cautioned his listeners not to put a protective barrier between themselves and the experience of life. Eck began to see that the way a person approached his or her own tradition could create such a barrier.

Eck started to widen her perspective on religion. She realized Christians do not have a monopoly on love, wisdom, and justice. She found ways to respect the rich Hindu tradition she encountered without feeling she had to discard her Christianity. She re-thought the meaning of Incarnation, seeing it now as God's presence in the lives of people of all faiths. Eck stepped off the edge of her existing spiritual map, but she remained rooted in the Christian tradition. She did this without trying to prove the superiority of Christianity or defending it against other religions.

One of the most profound experiences in Eck's dialogue with Hinduism moved her to a new level of appreciation for the mystery of God. The revelatory moment occurred when she attended the evening offering of lamps to Vishnu. She and a group of women lined up, waiting to be admitted to the temple service. While drums beat and bells clanged, an attendant admitted them to the inner sanctum.

The tempo and sound of the bells intensified, and then a pair of doors opened to reveal the central part of a sculpture of a reclining figure. Next the doors to the left opened to reveal the upper portion, and finally the doors to the right opened to reveal the third portion. As lamps were raised to cast light on each of these portions, Eck sensed an enormous presence. It was a presence more pervasive and encompassing than the individual huge sections of the figure. She found herself overwhelmed with the astounding immensity of God.

The image of Vishnu challenged Eck in a deeply personal way and enlarged her religious vision. She was challenged because she encountered the mystery of the divine through a culture older than

Christianity, in a Hindu temple where a Christian might not expect to encounter God. Her religious vision was enlarged because she was stretched not only intellectually but also emotionally by her life-altering confrontation with the mystery of an infinite God.

Experiences like Eck's show us that religious pluralism can enrich our appreciation and understanding of the mystery of God. While it is true that exposure to pluralism can lead some to wander rootless or become mired in relativism, it can also introduce new possibilities for understanding the hidden God. One way to avoid becoming rootless and relativistic is to remain in one tradition while exploring another. John Dunne speaks of this as "passing over" from one culture or religion to another.[4] "Passing over" may allow people to see religion with fresh eyes so that when they return to their own tradition they know it differently and, by knowing it differently, appreciate religious and spiritual insights they had neglected before.

"Passing over" suspends the desire to defend the God of one's own religion. Defense of one's beliefs is sometimes necessary, but it can also mask a variety of motives. When we defend the honor of God who is mystery we do not know for sure what we are defending. We may be defending our foremothers and forefathers who have committed themselves to the preservation of religious faith. We may be defending an idea of God that holds our world together. We may be defending ourselves.

Sometimes the instinct to defend tradition and God also arises from a desire for certainty about an idea of God. Certainty about our beliefs and ideas of God is hard to maintain in a changing culture; it can even get in the way of radical faith, which brings its own validation of the mystery of God. As a sense of mystery deepens, we may find we do not need to prove that our beliefs are truer than others' beliefs. We may also find we need not fear that we must "get it right" to have an honest relation with God.

Radical faith strips us clean of our ideas of God so that we are open to meet the God who is, not the God we prefer. The religious God—the God who dwells in churches, who likes pious prayers and speaks in pious language, who is always fair to people, especially those who do what is right, whose presence is clear and unmistakable—is not one we necessarily meet as we surrender to a radical faith.

The God we are more likely to meet in radical faith is the God whose whisper is heard in the midst of profound silence or whose touch is felt at moments when our usual defenses are down. The God we meet in radical faith is the God who is revealed in unlikely people and places. What makes this faith radical is that it is the bedrock that lies beneath our beliefs, our practices, our biases. The bedrock of faith is tested, among other places, in cultural climates characterized by ambiguity.

The Ability to Live in the Midst of Ambiguity

Simone Weil lived in a world that was not only secular but also pitted with conflicting claims to truth. Secular philosophy and science absorbed the attention of many intellectuals even as they ignored the horrors of war and the persecution of Jews. In this world one could easily trun to atheism, but not the intellectual Weil. She perceived a spiritual dimension that was not being articulated. Her radical faith enabled her to see a larger truth that could not be grasped by a single philosophy or single religious faith.

In one of her letters to Father Perrin, her spiritual friend, she recounts the development of the spirituality that drove her quest for truth. As an adolescent she went through a period of darkness. The darkness lifted when she was seized by the conviction that she could penetrate the kingdom of truth if she longed for it enough. She chose to concentrate all her attention on attaining that truth. She found compelling examples in the lives of Francis of Assisi and Jesus, as well as others, but their inspiration pointed her toward truth that dwells in inaccessible light, a truth that transcends ambiguity and the biases of religion.

Weil was not afraid to point out the religious biases of her spiritual friend. She respected Father Perrin but she criticized what she saw as his inability to see a picture of faith larger than Catholicism or traditional belief. She felt he could not understand that agnosticism was not an obstacle but that it had brought her to faith. She maintains that he equates the lack of orthodoxy with falsehood. She tells him that he has identified too much with the church as an earthly country where he lives attached to its human warmth. She is convinced that she is called to remain outside the institutional church, even in the midst of ambiguity, in order to affirm the vastness of truth scattered through the universe.

Weil clearly appreciates Father Perrin's friendship, but she hears different music. She will not give herself to a religion—though Catholicism attracts her—if she feels it closes itself off from the larger richness of God's love and truth. The truth she seeks is in the search, not in a final conclusion. She accepts that this position puts her at the margin where she must live as a kind of pilgrim. Without a lasting home she is free to explore ideas that would unsettle more conventional religious thinkers.

Weil's insights can be so shocking that they are easily dismissed. She does not use their shock value simply to jolt people out of their complacency. As a pilgrim and a mystic, Weil's reckless language comes from a deeper place. The hallmarks of her thinking—paradox, balanced critique, and the creative use of myth and symbol—are the tools of a mystic. Unlike nature mystics who see God as the underlying connection in the midst of great diversity, Weil envisions a God who unifies opposing truths. This gives her expression a paradoxical edge. Her mysticism is the unsettling mysticism of one who knows that the love of God calls all relative values into question and upsets conventional wisdom. It survives ambiguity and a host of contradictions.

Few of us could function in a position as solitary as Weil's. She wrestled with God without the aid of a supportive faith community. She did not align herself with any religious tradition. Had Weil lived a generation or two later, she would have found more people like herself who were willing to search for spiritual truth beyond the confines of a single religious tradition, while remaining rooted in it. She might have seen that being rooted in a tradition does not necessarily close a person off from the search for fuller truth. But despite her solitariness, she still has something to teach us.

Weil lived until the middle of World War II, largely in France which was becoming occupied by the Germans. At the same time, she lived in metaphorical "occupied territory." She was an outsider in a European culture whose dominant religious currents she could not claim as her own. The spiritual values she held put her at the margins of society's conventional value system.

We, too, sometimes feel we live symbolically in "occupied territory." The affluent, technological environment surrounding us seems to be controlled by forces that do not serve the values we espouse. The world we inhabit is full of the ambiguities of want in the midst of abundance and complacency in the midst of struggles for freedom and equality. Developed nations see themselves as lands of freedom, but they do not always promote moral and spiritual freedom. We live in places "occupied" by inhibiting cultural influences that are hostile to humanizing values and inner freedom.

The landscape we inhabit is full of landmines that make the search for God more difficult, but at the same time it presents us with unprecedented opportunities to shape our faith as we learn to find our truth in the midst of ambiguity. Both Eck and Weil searched for a truth that was not narrowly "objective." It was the kind of truth that requires the skill or ability to act without being driven by the need for immediate results.

The Ability to Act without Concern for Results

The poet Denise Levertov says every work of art is an "act of faith" in the sense of being a journey into the unknown.[5] Entering into that unknown brings artists in touch with truths that are larger than their individual "truths." But truth will not be discovered unless the artist acts before knowing where it will lead and without worrying about results.

Levertov says the artist must dive into waters whose depths have not been tested and hope that he or she will not be swallowed up or knocked out by crashing into a hard obstacle. When artists surrender to the call, they can rise and be buoyed up by it. They can discover what they could not have been known if they were concerned with a particular result.

To enter into the waters of faith, it is often as necessary to let go of questions as it is to have them. Often our questions are shaped by concerns posed by a culture that wants to eliminate mystery. Or sometimes they arise from a desire for clarity that cannot be met. When questions about faith are formulated to result in clear statements, they may simply provide a temporary life raft rather than encouraging us to plunge into the river of faith. There is a time to question and a time to refrain from questioning.

It was noted earlier that faith is not to be confused with belief. Beliefs are the propositions or statements we can put into words. Beliefs refer to our expressions *about* God, Jesus, church, world, and ourselves. People have sometimes said to me, "I think I am losing my faith. I don't know what I believe anymore." I try to ask them how this presumed lack of faith has affected their behavior. They often say they don't act any differently. They are still decent, caring people. They still believe that honesty is better than falsehood, and forgiveness is better than revenge. They may even still attend church. When they observe that they are losing their faith, they seem to be confusing individual beliefs that undergo all sorts of subtle changes with the bedrock of faith. The bedrock of faith keeps a person rooted in ultimate values though the winds of change may blow around them.

The winds of change may shake belief but will not shake what persons see as their intrinsic vocation or destiny. Action creates and reinforces a desire to embody certain values. This is what Levertov calls work that "enfaiths." For example, acting in love or acting in faith creates a climate for further action and insight into love or faith. The reason for acting is not to achieve a particular result but to affirm the intrinsic value of the action.

Others support what Levertov suggests about faith. They, too, hold that actions, rather than arguments, are what often lead persons to faith and sustain them more than words. In responding to his friend Robert Bridges who asked how he could increase his faith, Gerard Manley Hopkins said simply, "Give alms." What he meant was that Bridges should act in love so as to create a climate of faith. When Denise Levertov was unable to resolve her questions about

God, she found that acting in faith was what drew her into a relationship with God.

In corresponding with a student who was concerned that he was losing his faith, Flannery O'Connor cautioned him not to get so involved with intellectual difficulties.[6] He would have these all his life, she said, but he was too young to decide he didn't have faith just because he didn't believe. "About the only way we know whether we believe or not is by what we do," she said.

As the struggling priest says in Bernanos's *The Diary of a Country Priest*, we do not lose faith when we stop finding comfort in beliefs. We do not lose it the way we lose a set of keys. Radical faith remains so long as we live our lives in a direction that affirms life and the hope of a future, without withholding faith until we see results of action.

The Roots and Wings of Faith

Radical faith is the rock-bottom conviction that God is, despite challenges of other religions, the rise and fall of particular beliefs, the absence of feeling, or doubts about what faith is. This faith is not to be confused with beliefs, which are the intellectual expression of faith. It is surrender to an ultimate concern without the constant reassurance that our beliefs are unassailable. Most of us can't aspire to it in a vacuum. Radical faith seems most sustainable when it has roots as well as wings.

The roots of faith are found in the wisdom of religious tradition, the experiences and words of spiritual ancestors, and the support of a faithful community. For all that we might want to ignore these tangible expressions of faith because of their past and present failings, they remind us of something important. They let us know that our struggles are not new, that we have been shaped by a tradition of faith, that we are not self-sufficient, and that it is unlikely we can persevere in faith in the long run without being connected with others who seek God. As basic as radical faith might be, it is entwined in the roots that connect us to history.

Radical faith has wings as well. It does not cling to the forms it once had, but allows itself to mature as situations demand. Simone

Weil said that we must have the holiness demanded by the present moment, one involving a new type of sanctity.[7] To meet the challenge presented and to participate in this sanctity, Weil said, a new kind of genius is needed. She believes the genius will be given by God for the asking, but its demands are great. It will require new spiritual skills to meet the challenge. We have identified some of those challenges—pluralism, multiple truths, ambiguity, and the desire for results. To meet them we need the wings of radical faith.

Faith puts us in the path of God's light, but the intense light blinds us so we cannot see. Sometimes it doesn't seem like direct light at all but more like the dark new moon, the last phase of a waning moon and the beginning of a new one. But even that can instill hope. The moon waxes and wanes, but it never totally disappears. We do not see its farthest side, but it is ever-present like the radical faith that sustains us even when beliefs are shaken. What also sustains us is a contemplative spirit that guides the journey through faith. The next chapter takes up this theme.

13

Cultivating Skills of Contemplation

Ask someone what comes to mind when they hear the word *contemplation* and they are likely to associate it with reflection, meditation, deep prayer, light, and peace. Chances are they will also associate it with monks and nuns spending their days in silence and prayer, living out an ancient rhythm that ordinary people see as having little relevance for them. This narrow meaning describes an experience within a particular form of religious life, but there are other meanings that are deeper and broader—and that do not apply only to those who are professional religious.

Contemplation in its deepest sense refers to a prayerful receptivity to the Godhead without necessarily focusing on a specific image of God. It is different from meditation in that meditation involves reflection on a particular subject or aspect of God, while contemplation concerns a direct awareness of God. John of the Cross understands contemplation as the mode of prayer characterizing union with God, a union often marked by darkness and unknowing.[1]

This classic description captures the religious significance of contemplation. It refers most specifically to the prayer of union in which words and images are not as important as simple presence. At the same time, there is a broader meaning of contemplation based on the way a person approaches God or the world. In this sense we can speak of a contemplative attitude.

A contemplative attitude enables a person to face the world where God is hidden with openness, non-acquisitiveness, and an abiding sense that everything is connected. The cultivation of this attitude and its related skills can go a long way in helping us appreciate the presence of God within ordinary circumstances. It can also serve as an antidote for the frenzied pace of the environment in which we try to find God.

Our culture surrounds us with opportunities for distraction, self-protection, and gratification. These are not optimal conditions for encountering the subtle presence of a hidden God. A contemplative attitude opens one to God by quieting the demands of ego. It lessens the inclination of the ego to control, and teaches it to wait patiently for the stirring of the spirit. The contemplative attitude is more connected with not-doing than with doing.

The contemplative attitude has no goal but to be aware of the presence of a hidden Spirit. It breaks the hold of the busyness and distractions of the practical ego in the spiritual life as well as in ordinary life. As the hold of the practical ego is loosened, certain spiritual skills, like the ability to tolerate solitude and silence, grow.

A contemplative attitude involves a number of spiritual skills in addition to the ability to enjoy solitude and silence. Among these skills is the ability to embrace simplicity, to relinquish the need for an ideal self, to lay aside the usual defenses and guides, and to trust the presence of the sacred in the ordinary. Cultivating these skills can help develop the spiritual maturity needed to deal with a hidden God

Embracing Simplicity, Accepting What Is

There is a good market for simplicity these days, but one can't help wondering if it is really simplicity that is being promoted. Books and magazines that tell people how to live simply often promote a new form of consumerism. Gurus of organization equate simplicity with tidiness. The kind of simplicity that removes clutter from the soul has more to do with poverty of spirit and a contemplative attitude than with orderliness and a taste for the classic. Spiritual simplicity, like material simplicity, depends on the skill of knowing when to let go of what is useful to make room for what is essential. It doesn't take the deprivation of material poverty, but it does take something akin to poverty of spirit.

Simplicity and poverty of spirit are at the heart of a contemplative attitude. The poet Jane Kenyon was asked by Bill Moyers whether choosing the life of a poet requires poverty since a literary life does not promise financial security.[2] She responded that more than poverty, it requires a life of as much simplicity as possible. The simpler the life, the more one can be open to what the world presents rather than responding to it out of one's own desires.

Kenyon and her husband left the financial security of academic life to live in rural New Hampshire, where they found simplicity made possible what greater material comfort did not. It allowed them the time and environment to practice their craft of poetry and to become an intimate part of the community where they lived. It put them in touch with the most fundamental realities of life. It provided a context for Jane Kenyon to develop the contemplative skills that make her poetry so poignant.

Kenyon's poetry speaks of the ordinary rhythm of daily activities. The richness of her simple life shows through in the sense of loss she feels when she sees a stain on her dead grandmother's gravy boat or watches a man leave the hospital with his wife's coat. It makes itself known when she writes of the pleasure she takes in the fragrance of peonies. And it shines luminously in her poem "When Evening Comes," a contemplative tribute to the acceptance of life's movement. In this poem Kenyon describes the quieting of activity at the end of a day, closing each verse with a chant of simple acceptance, "Let evening come."

"Let it come." Kenyon writes these words from the depths of her own experience. She struggled with depression most of her life. She faced her husband's several bouts with cancer and eventually lost her own life to leukemia before she was fifty. Her poem testifies that in the midst of struggle the contemplative attitude teaches us to recognize what is gift, and not the result of our efforts. She says this poem came to her as a gift that "fell" out of her.

The poem's contemplative mood shows us how acceptance can quietly wash over concerns that dissipate energy. The poem shows us a steady vision that surfaces when the ego stops its striving. The ego has to learn to stop its striving, however, not just in the mundane activities of productive work and daily life. It has to learn to let go of its need to prove itself even in religious and moral matters.

Relinquishing the Need for an Ideal Self

Even sincerely religious persons can get caught up in subtle ego preoccupations. Richard Foster was serious about his religion and gave himself selflessly and wholeheartedly to it. He said "yes" to any reasonable request for his service. But the active religious speaker and author found himself overextended because of all the obligations he had taken on.[3]

Foster was frustrated at not being able to fulfill all his commitments to his satisfaction. He appeared confident and competent, but he was feeling stretched to the limit, tired and scattered. Sitting in an airport one rainy morning, he passed the time reading. What he read from Thomas Kelly's *Testament of Devotion* unsettled and yet inspired him.

Foster read, "We feel honestly the pull of many obligations and try to fulfill them all. And we are unhappy, uneasy, strained, oppressed, and fearful we shall be shallow. . . . We have hints that there is a way of life vastly richer and deeper than all this hurried existence, a life of unhurried serenity and peace and power. If only we could slip over into that Center." Foster recognized himself in this description. He knew he had to do something. Right there he committed himself to learn to say no to some of the many worthwhile commitments he was in the habit of accepting.

The next time he had the opportunity to act on his decision, he did. He declined the request of the next person who sought his help without offering an explanation to justify the refusal. The apparently insignificant event became a turning point that led not only to a less hurried existence but also to greater self-knowledge.

Foster recognized, at a level deeper than his frustration at being too busy, that he was being affected by something other than the needs of others. He had allowed himself to get caught in a daily routine controlled by his need to be useful. The obstacle to a more centered relationship with God was not pride or selfish concerns of the ego. What kept him from being centered contemplatively was his *idea* of self, his functional ego. He had become the slave of an acceptable religious self. His challenge was to let go of the ideal self that was holding him hostage so that he could be open to what each situation required, even if it was to do nothing.

So many ideas of God are tangled up with an idea of the self that relates to God. What does God expect of me? How can I show God I am serious about my spiritual life? How can I become a better person? These are still ego questions even though they are not obviously self-serving. They are full of the illusion of an ideal self. The ideal self is not likely to bring us to conscious awareness of union with God. It depends too much on our own efforts to maintain and nourish it. Recognition of an existing relationship with God eliminates the need for an ideal self.

A contemplative attitude disposes us to forget the project of creating an ideal self that deserves God's favor. It moves us beyond the desire to earn love by being useful, devoted, or worthy because it focuses on union with something larger than self. A contemplative attitude opens us to the presence of God (and the deepest self)— both beyond affirmation or negation. Openness to that presence often takes laying aside the usual instruments of the quest for God.

Laying Aside the Usual Instruments

The power of a contemplative attitude sometimes becomes evident in surprising places. One of William Faulkner's stories illustrates a contemplative attitude through an extended metaphor. "The Bear" serves as a parable for the art of encountering the elusive presence of God.[4] In the story, Ike McCaslin, a ten-year-old boy, joins a group of men who hunt regularly for quail and deer, but set their sights ultimately on a legendary bear, Old Ben.

During the second week of one of their hunts, after the dogs burst into a cacophony of yelps, a man tells Ike that they have sighted Ben. He says that every year Old Ben nears the camp to see who has newly arrived and whether they can shoot or not. The boy, fearful and fascinated, now knows himself as being sized up and, in some sense, hunted.

The man teaches Ike to track the bear by listening and looking until he senses that the bear, whom he cannot see, knows he is there. This awakens an even stronger desire in Ike to be able to really look at Old Ben. He works to develop his abilities but does not see the bear that season. When Ike returns the following year, having fine-tuned his skills, he finds he is still not catching a glimpse of the mythic bear. His mentor tells him that the gun can no longer serve as the tool of the trade. The bear is put off by it. So one day Ike ventures out without it, armed only with a stick and a compass.

After pursuing his quarry a while, Ike considers that surrendering the gun may not have been enough. Maybe the bear requires that he leave behind all self-protection and all instruments of direction. He hangs the compass on a bush and places the stick next to it, and enters deeper into the forest.

As Ike follows the bear's tracks deeper into the woods, he suddenly sees Old Ben in an open space. The animal simply appears, large and almost immobile. Its mysterious presence overwhelms him. Just being there is enough. He realizes that his goal has changed since he first heard of Ben and wanted to join in the hunt. He is no longer hunting the animal. He has no purpose but to encounter it. The encounter is brief, and the bear soon begins to leave the glade. It is highlighted briefly by the sunlight before it returns to the obscurity of the forest. Before the bear leaves, Ike sees it cast a backward glance toward him. It leaves as it arrived—in mystery.

The reader, too, has been allowed a brief glimpse into mystery, and has learned an important lesson about the conditions for encountering mystery. The lesson is that when it comes to meeting the unknown, whether a strange animal or the hidden God, our usual approaches and aids will not likely serve well.

The usual skills of religious searchers—conventional worship, church affiliation, saying prayers, personal sacrifices—offer no guarantee that the presence of God will be encountered. These practices are very useful for certain aspects of the journey, but when the presence of God seems more hidden, they may not bring the desired results. These practices unite us with a community of faith that supports trust in the hidden God. But each God-seeker will have to learn to trust the hidden God in his or her own way. Each person will need to cultivate skills of letting go of his or her defenses and compasses.

Familiar defenses like the tendency to calculate risk, the anticipation of desired outcomes, and the fear of vulnerability—all keep the spiritual explorer from venturing freely into the unknown and learning to trust. At some point it becomes clear that they are impeding relationship with God. But letting go of stubborn habits of survival is never easy, especially when we haven't considered letting go as a skill that can be developed.

Ike has a lesson to teach us about the skill of letting go. He sets his sights on the bear, forgetting himself. He lets himself be swept up in the adventure, letting go of defensive habits of heart. He puts ego concerns aside. He surrenders to the call to track the trackless presence.

"The Bear," like the stories of Job and Moses, tells us we cannot control God. We still try. We turn God from a polar bear into a teddy bear, so we can be safe from the awesome uncertainty of what we might meet. We devise a household deity to fit our personal needs and to minimize risk. We domesticate God to avoid facing our illusions, and we create a buffer against the mystery of God. As long as we try to control or second-guess God, God will elude us.

God will also elude us if we think a contemplative attitude means we will be led to God through lofty spiritual thoughts and feelings. On the contrary, one of the most basic skills of a contemplative attitude is the ability to trust the ordinary as the site of God's presence.

Trusting the Ordinary

Monastic life over the centuries has been the training site for contemplative skills like the abilities to live simply, in silence, and in solitude. Because of the rarefied monastic atmosphere, people have tended to romanticize the meaning of contemplation. They have imagined it to involve a more or less constant heightened state of mystical awareness. Contrary to this way of thinking, a contemplative attitude, even in a monastic setting, has much more to do with the ordinary than with the extraordinary. Mark Salzman makes this evident in his novel *Lying Awake.*

Lying Awake tells the story of Sister John of the Cross, a Carmelite nun who, after a long period of spiritual dryness, begins to experience the intensity of God's presence.[5] In the early years of her religious life Sister John of the Cross fulfilled her duties faithfully but did not feel joy or consolation. The rhythm of work and prayer went on day after day without the intimacy with God she had hoped for. The love she pursued seemed to elude her. Yet she never considered leaving religious life because she felt she would no longer fit in a world that does not recognize God. The life she chose has been, and it seems will be, a vast empty desert.

Then, after thirteen years, she suddenly has a breakthrough. God is vividly present to her in an extraordinary way. Prayer becomes joyful, and the presence of God vivid. Her poetic abilities begin to bloom, and her talents are recognized beyond her monastery. She revels in the intensity of her experience and sees it as the culmination of years of waiting. Everything is the same, but everything is miraculously different. Faithfulness to her commitment evolves into a deeply satisfying spiritual life.

But this blossoming of spiritual intensity is soon to be shaken. Though she is enjoying her consoling religious transformation, she has developed chronic headaches and blurred vision. The problem causes the other sisters great concern, and she agrees to visit a neurologist for some tests. The neurologist explains that she has a small tumor that is causing her neurological problems. Surgery is necessary to correct them.

The surgeon tells her the meningioma can produce different symptoms for different people, among them an altered state of consciousness that absorbs a person into another world of meaning. This may be the reason for her transformative religious experience. The tumor can be removed easily, but the altered state of consciousness she has enjoyed will probably disappear.

She speaks with her spiritual guides about the decision she has to make. With the surgery she will no longer have headaches and other symptoms, but she will also lose the extraordinary enjoyment of God's company and probably her poetic gifts. Without the surgery she may hold on to her bliss longer, but then what?

After anguishing over the decision, she decides to have the surgery, but she wonders the night before the surgery whether she will be changed afterward, and what she will do if she can no longer think clearly or cannot write or read. Most important, she wonders what will happen if she comes out of the surgery thinking her vocation is as false as her visions now seem to be.

Sister John lets the truth of her relationship with God win out. In an act of radical faith and trust, she demonstrates that she does not need extraordinary visions or consolation, but only God. She relinquishes the contemplation she has known for another kind.

When she recovers from her surgery, she resumes ordinary daily life. Her poetic gift is no longer evident, but she finds her humdrum daily life solid and reassuring. She sharpens her contemplative skills by observing the oldest and the newest members living out the same quotidian mystery that she lives. She doesn't look for something more. She realizes she does not need more than the nourishment ordinary life already provides. Her trust in the sacredness of the ordinary, a skill she had quietly built over the years, enables her to continue to express a contemplative attitude.

There are more obvious skills connected with a contemplative attitude than those we have considered—the ability to listen in silence and solitude, to persevere in prayer, to focus single-mindedly on God, to note a few—but these may not be the place to start if God seems hidden. The skills examined in this chapter, as well as a number we have not examined, serve as a kind of reorientation for those of us who search for the hidden God in a new landscape. These less overtly religious skills help us to still ourselves so that we can orient ourselves toward a God who beckons in new ways and in new places. These spiritual skills also help create a disposition for the cultivation of other skills. One of those skills, the deepening of self-knowledge, is the topic of the next chapter.

14

Cultivating Skills of Self-Knowledge

The value of self-knowledge has a long history in Western culture. From Plato's statement that the unexamined life is not worth living to Polonius's exhortation "to thine own self be true," self-understanding has been seen as central to a person's full stature as a human being.

Self-knowledge begins in self-awareness and ends in self-transcendence. Self-awareness is the consciousness of our inner states—our feelings, moods, thoughts, and biases. Self-awareness pertains first to a given moment. It is not always easy to be aware of what is going on in ourselves or others, especially while it is happening. Daniel Goleman writes that much of our emotional life does not cross the threshold into conscious awareness.[1] The first work in self-knowledge is learning to observe our reactions by a slight stepping back from experience so that we can not only know our moods but also understand our thoughts about them.

When we are aware and when we can see a pattern in our self-awareness, we can begin to develop the kind of self-knowledge that allows the examination of our life and the ability to be true to our deepest self. Self-knowledge goes beyond the moment to illuminate one's personal history. Self-knowledge allows us to know not only what we think, feel, want, or fear at a given point in life; it also allows us to see patterns and the role that particular thoughts, feelings, and desires play in the totality of who we are. That includes knowing how we have changed and how we have stayed the same.

Spiritual self-knowledge takes basic self-knowledge a step further. It allows us to see ourselves in a context larger than the immediate situation. It enables us to choose the direction of our lives, the way we relate to others, and the quality of our relationship with God. Spiritual self-knowledge calls for spiritual skills such as the ability to act out of an awareness of our own dignity and to love others as ourselves, to take responsibility for our moral failures and seek forgiveness, to forgive others who have failed, and to reach out to others in compassion.

It is hard to know others if we do not know ourselves. But it is also hard to know ourselves if we do not know others. The skills of self-knowledge are not just individual; they are interpersonal and transpersonal as well. The fulfillment of self-knowledge comes in self-transcendence, which is the realization that self is more than the individual ego, more than just what we experience at a given moment or even over a longer period. The fulfillment of self-knowledge comes in the realization that *self* means self-in-relation, not just an individual who is center of the universe. Self-transcendence makes it possible to forget the self by loving, forgiving, or acting in true justice. It testifies that each of us is part of a greater whole in which God is hidden.

Each of these paths to self-identity—self-awareness, self-knowledge, and self-transcendence—develops through the exercise of certain emotional abilities, including the ability to listen without defensiveness and to make connections, and certain spiritual abilities, including the ability to practice humility and compassion. We often take these skills for granted, as if they develop on their own without needing to be cultivated. In a few gifted individuals they seem to develop naturally, but for most of us the skills of self-knowledge have to be cultivated more deliberately.

As we try to identify and cultivate spiritual skills of self-knowledge, we all face challenges from the culture we live in and from our own personal dispositions. While culture puts some obstacles in the way of genuine self-knowledge by offering incentives to create a culturally acceptable self, we are ultimately responsible for our own destiny. We can't blame culture for our lack of self-knowledge, any more than we can blame it for our lack of faith or lack of attentiveness. Culture can make these harder, but in the final analysis it is up to us to develop skills of self-knowledge.

In the following sections we will explore several skills that contribute to growth in self-knowledge and self-transcendence. The ones we will examine are the skills of honesty and humility, empathy and forgiveness, and transforming pain into love. These skills can be seen in the stories of several individuals who grew in self-understanding by opening themselves to a larger world of relations. Their stories reveal that genuine self-knowledge often comes about, directly or indirectly, by allowing ourselves to be touched by a world larger than ourselves.

Skills of Honesty and Humility

By definition, a skill involves the ability to use one's knowledge effectively. People may have self-awareness of a personal quality such as the ability to exercise leadership, but they need skills to put it into action. When it comes to leadership, honesty and humility about one's strengths and weaknesses are essential skills if one is to lead well.

Robert Coles was interested in the roots and exercise of moral leadership, so he decided to interview a number of people, including Dorothy Day, founder of the Catholic Worker Movement.[2] His interviews revealed, among other things, the spiritual skill of honesty that Day consciously cultivated. That skill was fostered through the encouragement of a trusted confidant who helped her know herself better.

In the interviews, Dorothy Day revealed that she did not see herself as totally independent in developing her leadership abilities. Day wanted to make it clear that her moral leadership was not an isolated gift for which she alone could take credit. The leadership gifts she knew she had needed to be tested and made effective; for that she depended a great deal on the mentoring of her moral and spiritual guide, Peter Maurin.

Peter Maurin was a simple French peasant whose personality and approach were quite different from Day's. She was the visible leader of the Catholic Worker Movement and the *Catholic Worker* newspaper that promoted its ideals. But he was the visionary who got them going and kept them going. And it was he who helped her understand more radically who she was.

Maurin had a powerful influence on Day's self-knowledge. Day observed that Maurin had the ability to move "mountains of pride, of self-absorption," and to dispel the isolation created by her competing interests. Maurin was willing to help her confront the obstacles that kept her, and others, from doing what was needed.

The obstacles Day had to face were not obstacles of inertia or hesitation. Day, the activist, knew what needed doing. But she needed help in understanding others and herself better. She needed to identify her feelings, weigh their intensity, and see what she could learn from them. She needed to understand the perspectives of others and to find ways to communicate with sensitivity. She needed to see her efforts as part of a larger spiritual picture.

Maurin possessed an emotional intelligence and spirit of freedom sometimes more acute than Dorothy Day's. From Maurin's insights, Day grew to recognize the subtle involvement of ego that could enter even her generous efforts to help others and change society. In her pursuit of God, and an ideal self, she could get caught up in concerns that obscured her true self.

Dorothy Day was self-effacing about her leadership; she clearly exhibited leadership skills, but she also was aware they did not exist in some pure state unrelated to her personal agenda. Coles learned of Day's awareness of the "darker side" of her altruism: her arrogance, potential self-righteousness, irritability, and desire for privacy. When she faced this darker side, she realized it could not be dealt with through psychoanalysis. Deep self-knowledge could come only from spiritual wisdom.

Day saw self-understanding as a step toward forgiveness. If she could find reasons to forgive herself, she felt she was better able to take on the world. She trusted that the sacrament of confession could better lead her to a radical spiritual self-understanding. But on a day-to-day basis, it was Maurin who was the catalyst for helping her see herself more honestly and for experiencing forgiveness. Without the visionary Peter Maurin, the activist Dorothy Day might not have come to know her ego-self as honestly as she did.

Maurin was a kind of "geologist of the soul" who helped Day to know herself better by teaching her to recognize the hidden vulnerable spots where she was likely to meet God. The term "geologist of the soul" has been used to describe the work of a spiritual guide.[3] Someone once asked a Lubavitcher rabbi what he was good for. He answered the question by describing a teacher who exemplified for him what the rabbi should do for others.

> "I'm not talking about myself, I'm talking about what my master was for me. He was for me the geologist of the soul. There are great treasures in the soul; there's faith, there's love, there's wisdom, all these treasures you can dig, but if you don't know where to dig, you dig up mud—Freud—or you dig up stones—Adler. But if you want to get to the gold, which is the awe before God, and the silver, which is the love, and the diamonds, which is the faith, then you have to find the geologist of the soul who tells you where to dig." The rebbe added, "But the digging you have to do for yourself."

Peter Maurin showed Dorothy Day where to dig. As the rabbi said, if a person has a guide, they get a better sense of how to direct their personal effort. When individuals lack a guide, they must sometimes wait a long time until they are ready to discover the spiritual skills they need.

Skills of Empathy and Forgiveness

In his memoir *The Blessing*, Gregory Orr describes how an experience of tragedy eventually brought him to new self-understanding. He recounts his long struggle with guilt over having caused his brother's death.[4] As a twelve-year-old on a hunting trip with his father, Orr accidentally shot and killed his eight-year-old brother. After his initial horror, he was inconsolable. His mother tried to reach out to reassure him by telling him something never discussed before or after. His father had killed a friend in a hunting accident when he was about ten. The revelation did not console Greg.

Later when his father's receptionist came to see him, she tried to offer him religious solace. "This is an awful thing, Greg, but you should know that right now Peter is in heaven with Jesus." He wanted to scream at her, "This isn't Sunday school! My brother was just killed by a bullet and I fired it. What kind of nonsense are you saying?" She continued, "It may not make sense now, . . . but it's all part of God's plan."

Orr says he hadn't thought of God much before, but these words had the opposite effect of what was intended. The words ended any possibility of conventional religious belief because they made a mockery of what he had seen and done.

Years later as he set out to write of the event that changed everything, he remembers a dream in which he envisioned himself as the biblical Cain who killed his brother. He says that dream originally gave meaning to his experience because it placed him at the center of the story. But in time he came to realize the limits of putting himself at the center of the story. Other people, including his parents, had their own stories to deal with their grief. He had not tried to put himself in their place to understand what they might be feeling.

The way Orr told his story had conditioned the way he saw himself. He was the center of the drama, the one burdened with guilt. When he allowed himself to widen his view by entering the stories of his parents, this conditioning loosened its grip on him. He was no longer the sole focus. He was able to transcend his own experience to enter into theirs.

Orr's father, a week before the shooting, had ignored his own father's warning about the danger of having guns around the house when there were children. His mother, who first said the two younger boys should not go on the hunting trip, weakened and said to her husband, "maybe they could go just this one time." Each of them had a burden of guilt. Each could have acted otherwise.

Orr comes to realize the effect of neglecting his parents' versions of the story. "In my child's egoism, I couldn't realize my parents had lives and fates of their own, distinct from mine. It never occurred to me that they might believe that their own actions had brought them to this place." He grew to understand himself as someone who held on to his guilt by holding on to his own version of the story. This also prevented him from forgiving himself. He also learned the skill of empathy when he began to appreciate the pain of his parents because they had a different version of the story.

So, too, in a variety of ways, we narrow our focus to maintain our place at the center of the universe. We never really leave our child's egoism behind. Childhood egoism is just the beginning of an egoism we carry through life, even while we are learning to transcend it. We do move off our place at the center of things from time to time, but rarely is that move permanent or complete. Orr, who articulates what transcendence of ego meant for him, helps us to understand one of the skills we need to mature in our self-knowledge beyond the ego to a larger self.

Eventually Gregory Orr found a way to deal with his guilt and grief through art. Orr discovered the work of the sculptor David Smith. On a trip to Smith's workplace, he encountered art's "way of fighting." This was not to do battle but to stand very still. It was first to assume a contemplative attitude. By moving off the dead center of ego, one could learn to live and exult. Orr felt Smith's sculpture gave testimony to this contemplative attitude and its ability to move one beyond the narrow self. "The sculptor was dead. But what he had created moved on beyond him, proclaiming some powerful, mysterious significance."

Orr chose to make poems rather than sculpture. Like other forms of art, poetry allows him to celebrate the larger story of life that goes on despite his limitations, the passage of time, and the perishing of people. What he has learned, through the skills he developed, in particular through his ability to connect with others, becomes part of the ceaselessly flowing stream of life. Another skill of self-knowledge serves a similar purpose, the ability to transform pain into service.

Skills of Transforming Pain into Love

Love finds immediate and obvious expression, as it should, in the affectionate care we give to family and close friends. But the spiritually wise tell us it shouldn't stop there. Human beings are capable of a more radical love, one that concerns itself with the best interests of all human beings, whether they are part of one's own group or not. We might wonder what it takes to love in this way and how it is related to self-knowledge.

Liking others requires no special skills; it comes naturally. Loving does require skills. This is evident in Erich Fromm's definition of love as "the active concern for the life and growth of that which we love."[5] "Active concern" means we use spiritual intelligence and practice to foster our desire that others should live and grow. We develop skillful ways to affirm their value. Everyone does not have the same desire to work at developing the skills of love, and certainly everyone does not feel the need to express them universally. What do those who love widely have that others lack?

This was a question Samuel Oliner asked. Oliner was the beneficiary of the love of strangers who were moved by his pain, and when he in turn was moved by the pain of others and wanted to alleviate it, he dealt with it creatively. Oliner set out to make public the work of altruists and to discover why some people were more likely to express universal love and others were not.

Oliner, a sociologist at a college in northern California, began to teach a course on the Holocaust in 1977. He had heard that some people were denying it had happened, and he wanted to set the record straight. As Oliner worked through the material, he began to relive painful experiences from his own past. His memoir *Restless Memories* recounts those experiences.[6]

When he was twelve years old, he lived with his family in a small town in southeastern Poland. One day a convoy of Nazi trucks drove into town and began rounding up all the Jews in his ghetto. Oliner's mother urged him to run away and hide as soldiers began beating people and loading them into trucks. Still in his pajamas, Schmulek, as he was known then, went to the roof of their house and hid under boards and rubbish. He hid there all day until well after the town had been emptied. When he returned to the house for clothes, there was nothing there, but he managed to find something to wear in another house. He made his way to town where he knew a Gentile who had been on good terms with his father. He was admitted to the family's home, where he told his story and was given refuge.

It was clear that Schmulek should not stay there because he would be discovered, so the mother hastily prepared him to pass as a Gentile by teaching him a few prayers and fundamentals of catechism while urging him to be sure no one ever saw that he was circumcised. Then she gave him another name and sent him well into the back hills to work as a stable hand. There he was unlikely to be found. He told his employer he was earning money for his destitute family.

When the war was over, the woman sent her son to get Schmulek with the story that his mother was ill. Oliner left his refuge and began a long journey that took him to England as an orphan, to the United States where a relative sponsored his immigration, and finally to the West Coast where after a series of jobs he completed his Ph.D. at 41.

Oliner did not confront the pain he had experienced until he was 48 and teaching the course on the Holocaust. He discovered that his non-Jewish students were also pained by the events. When he tried to reassure a German student that the Nazis, not the Germans, were responsible for incredible acts of hatred, he realized the fuller picture had to be painted. Stories of brave rescuers needed to be told as well the stories of the cruel persecutors. He embarked on a long project of researching altruism during the Holocaust.

In the process of researching many aspects of altruism, Oliner and his wife tried to identify traits that distinguished those who were likely to help strangers from those who were not. The task proved to be harder than they thought. Phenomena of altruism were complex and varied. The qualities that seemed likely to correlate, like religiosity and self-esteem, turned out not to be significant. Other qualities surfaced slowly.

Oliner looked at factors like having a network of people to support altruism, having lived near to or having known Jews, and having a sense of autonomy to act independently. These factors were somewhat significant. So was the rescuers' capacity for empathy and their sense of personal and social responsibility. But the most significant factors in distinguishing rescuers from non-rescuers were closeness to a parent who was a role model and how far outside one's own group the rescuers saw others as like them. In the case of rescuers of

Jews and non-rescuers, then, the willingness to put themselves at risk depended strongly on the power of good family example and the cultivation of an expansive view of the human family. Samuel Oliner exemplified the skill of transforming pain into love. It is a skill that reinforces what we learned earlier in this chapter, namely that knowledge of self can be deepened through interaction with others. There are many ways to foster the process of gaining greater self-knowledge. We have caught glimpses of the process as we saw Dorothy Day's exercise of honesty in her relationships, as we witnessed how Gregory Orr's empathy for his parents helped relieve his guilt, and as we observed Samuel Oliner turn his awareness of compassion into research that benefits others.

The spiritual skills involved in gaining self-knowledge do not have a narcissistic goal. They reveal instead that we know ourselves most fully when we discover not an isolated ego, but a larger self. They also reveal that often others help us to grow in self-knowledge. We cannot say we know ourselves fully until we can say we know ourselves as connected to the rest of humanity and share in its weaknesses and its strengths, its joys and its pain. In the midst of that web of connections, it is quite possible we may meet the hidden God.

15

Awakening to a Hidden God

The goal of our exploring, T. S. Eliot said at the end of the *Four Quartets*, is to arrive where we started and to know the place for the first time.[1] As we conclude this phase of the exploration of a hidden God, it serves us well to take his words to heart. If we have been changed by the exploration, we will find ourselves where we began, at a new threshold of faith.

When we stand at a threshold, we are sometimes poised to enter a place that is already known. But the threshold of faith is not the entrance into something known; instead it is an entrance into the unknown. Before we began our exploration of the hidden God, we may have thought we knew the ways in which God is hidden; but after listening to our spiritual ancestors and the challenges of imaging God, we understand what it means in a different way. We appreciate the need for new skills to live with a God who remains hidden in our particular world.

The spiritual skills needed to live with a hidden God are the skills of living a threshold life, a life on the brink. Living at the threshold puts us at the edge of ordinary observation where the customary ways of knowing are suspended. Knowledge becomes more oblique and indirect. We become attuned not just to what is before us, but also to what is over the shoulder, at the edge of the visual field, or at the threshold of sound. There is no easy way to say how the focus shifts; it just becomes more relaxed and freer. There is less picking and choosing of what is important.

On-the-brink attentiveness is crucial, including attentiveness to a God who cannot be spoken of in clear and distinct ideas. Like the swampy margin between water and land, the intersection between human and divine eludes clear definitions. It requires us to watch where we are stepping and to pay attention to everything. The unfamiliar territory of the threshold presents an opportunity for learning the kind of attentiveness unlikely when everything is familiar. This is not the kind of attentiveness where a person knows exactly what he or she is looking for. The kind of attentiveness needed is a relaxed and open attentiveness that is able to wait for what comes as grace.

To wait for grace is to wait as a naturalist or as a poet, not as a scientist or a journalist. The naturalist lingers, almost nonchalantly, while nature unfolds to reveal its beauty and its secrets. The poet, too, waits as for an image or a phrase to ripen and drop its fruitful meaning. At the threshold there is no predetermined plan for what will be found. A boy tracking a mysterious bear and a birdwatcher hoping to see something unusual know it can be more useful to loiter and stroll. They know that what they hope to see does not show up at an appointed time.

Each moment is the threshold of a new moment. The life of faith is a life of always being on the brink, always at the verge of a first-time encounter for which there is no blueprint. Life is a series of first-time encounters, 86,400 seconds a day. When we assume the next moment will be like the last, the focus of attentiveness is lost. T. S. Eliot recognizes that the rediscovery of attentiveness is the poet's key to the door of faith. Thomas Merton also found that attentiveness, without interpretation, brought him to the brink of a new faith in the hidden God.

Awakening to a Hidden God

The evolution of Thomas Merton's thought from enthusiastic convert to social critic and ecumenical dialogue partner signals his movement into unfamiliar territory. The unfamiliar territory of Eastern religions, which he had begun to explore through reading and correspondence, became the place where he experienced a surprising revelation of the hidden presence of God. This revelation occurred during his journey to Asia not long before he died.[2]

Merton traveled to Asia in 1968. He went there to attend a conference and to meet with contemplatives of Eastern religious traditions. While he was there, Merton was eager to see the caves at Polonnaruwa in Sri Lanka with their frescoes and statues of the Buddha. He got a guide to take him, along with the vicar general of the diocese, so that he could see and photograph these ancient spiritual treasures.

After viewing a cave at Dambulla, they moved on to a spot at Gal Vihara where at the opening into a cave there were three huge Buddhas. On the left a large Buddha sat, while on the right there was a big Buddha reclining with another standing at its head. In the cave was another seated Buddha. The vicar general was uncomfortable with things "pagan" and stayed back while Merton moved forward to inspect the statues more carefully. It was then that he experienced a profound sense of presence he had never known before.

As Merton approached the Buddhas barefoot, walking through the wet grass and sand, he absorbed the silence of the extraordinary faces with their great smiles. They were colossal and yet provocatively subtle, filled with every possibility. Merton says they were simply there, questioning nothing, knowing everything, rejecting nothing. They exuded a peace that came not from emotional resignation but from an emptiness that has seen through every question without discrediting or refuting anything, without establishing a position. He was overwhelmed by a sense of gratitude for the obvious clarity of the figures, their shape and line, and the monumental bodies visible from many angles. His attentiveness, without religious interpretation, brought him to an extraordinary breakthrough.

Merton says the experience jerked him out of his habitual vision of things toward an exploding inner clarity. It was as if all mystery had dissolved and all problems resolved not because he had somehow discovered the "answers" to his questions but because now everything became evident to him in its ordinariness and emptiness; he saw that everything is compassion.

Merton goes on to say that he doesn't know when in his life he had such a sense of beauty and spiritual validity running together in one aesthetic illumination. The only time he had suggested something like it was when he described an episode on a street corner in Louisville where he had an overpowering sense of the unity of all humanity and his joy at being an ordinary part of it. The experience at Polonnaruwa, however, opened up a level of truth that did not call for Christian interpretation to clarify it. It was so complete in itself that he didn't have to embrace Buddhism or reject Christianity.

He confessed that the experience purified his Asian pilgrimage and made it clearer. Now that he sensed what he was looking for, he could not imagine what might remain to be discovered. There was nothing more to long for, and nothing to repudiate. Strangely, Merton's accidental death in Thailand occurred shortly after this penetrating experience.

Merton didn't use the word *God* in describing his experience. He didn't have to. Besides, to use the word would conjure up a sea of associations that would obscure the immediacy of his encounter. Merton encountered the mystery of existence de-mystified, and he encountered it away from the structured silence of a Cistercian monastery and away from the symbols of his Christian heritage. His encounter revealed that discovering the hidden God is not about *having an experience*. Discovering God is about the *transparency of experience*, about accepting with utter conviction that God *is*, despite our accumulated beliefs about who God is. The presence of God manifests itself in the transparency of experience when we are truly ready to encounter it. When that is we cannot know because the movement is part of our secret life.

The Secret Life

The secret life seems to be a recurring theme in much contemporary writing. We can read of the secret life of plants, of bees, even of dust. It seems some writers tell of the secret lives of things in order to show that they can be understood, that the mystery can be exposed and we need no longer be at the mercy of forces beyond our control. The reassurance is misleading. Some of what is hidden in secret must remain hidden. This is certainly true of God. Instead of looking for explanations to dispel the mystery of God, we would do better to respect God's hidden influence in our own lives. We would benefit more by seeking to grow in wisdom to discern the subtle movement that stirs us to move toward and away from God.

The great importance of subtle and hidden movement should not surprise us. One of the great lessons we learn from the age in which we live is that everything around and within us is teeming with movement invisible to our ordinary senses. Atoms and sub-atomic particles escape our observation. Almost imperceptible changes in the environment build up to produce cataclysmic events. Small discontent grows in cities and nations until revolution erupts. The mind processes new experiences and suddenly we no longer see things as we once did. Most of what is spiritually important—love, grief, hope, and hopelessness—works under the surface of daily activity, changing us steadily in small and secret ways. If we pay attention, one day we awake to realize we have had a secret life, unknown even to us.

Our secret lives can help us to accept God as hidden. At several points in the process of working on this book, I caught myself thinking about how audacious it is of me to write about God. It didn't take long for me to remind myself that I wasn't really writing about God, whose mystery must remain hidden. I was writing about how different people regard and relate to God. The impulse to regard and relate to God arises from the mystery of our own secret lives, which also are hidden. This gives rise to wonder.

Wonder is characteristic of those at the brink, say at the edge of a vast ocean. The ocean overruns the land, and the ocean recedes from it. There is nothing practical to be done about the movement of the sea. Wonder replaces the air of grave purposefulness that colors the daily lives of those who are earnestly looking for their version of something.

Waiting at the edge of infinity requires nothing of us but to be present and to witness in wonder. At this brink where we dwell on the boundary between the visible and the invisible, between the utterable and the unutterable, wonder resolves the tension between speech and silence. Wonder respects the secrets at the depths of the ocean, which if visible would no longer be ocean, as God without a hidden life would no longer be God.

Our secret lives give rise not only to wonder but also to prayer. Each life is a prayer, an utterance of joy, of lament, of longing, of celebration. Within each life the roots of joy, lament, longing, and celebration are hidden far beneath the momentary occasions that trigger them. Prayer is the impulse to claim our lives, to accept and affirm what is, even in the face of what we do not and cannot know. It is the song of those who stand at the threshold of faith and enter again and again.

If, as Eliot says, the goal of exploring is to arrive at where we started and to know the place for the first time, there is reason to celebrate. There is reason to celebrate because we have come to appreciate more fully that God is a hidden God who will not let us be duped into confusing our pious thoughts and feelings about God with God. There is reason to celebrate because the hidden God presents us with an opportunity to grow spiritually as we would not through our own choosing. There is reason to celebrate because, as Merton observed, we are being called to a level of prayer and meditation that is appropriate for who we are now and for the age in which we live.

Who we are now is not who we were when we first came to believe in God, and the age in which we live is not the age in which our traditional beliefs were formulated. We need no longer lament that God seems more hidden now. We can stop looking for God in a carefully preserved and beautifully wrapped package.

The presence of God rarely appears in a beautifully wrapped box that has our name on it and that says "from God." God appears in one guise after another, in one unexpected opportunity after another. The gift is often not apparent until the opportunity and the moment have passed. But by continuing our exploration of the hidden God, we can hope to get a little better at recognizing the unwrapped gift of God's presence and graciously receiving it with the gratitude of one who receives it for the first time. We can learn to say not only "thank you," but also "amen."

Notes

1. The "Disappearing" God

[1] Thomas Merton, *Contemplation in a World of Action* (Garden City, NY: Doubleday, 1973), 177–178.

[2] George Gallup Jr., *Religion in America, 1996* (Princeton, NJ: Princeton Religious Research Center, 1996). See also George Gallup Jr. and Jim Castelli, *The People's Religion* (New York: Macmillan, 1989), 252.

[3] Denise Levertov, "Flickering Mind," in *The Stream and the Sapphire* (New York: New Directions, 1997), 15–16.

[4] Jalal al-Din Rumi, *The Glance: Songs of Soul-Meeting*, trans. Coleman Barks with Nevit Ergin (New York: Penguin, 1999), 1.

[5] Thomas Merton, *Thoughts in Solitude* (Garden City, NY: Doubleday, 1956), 81.

[6] Thomas Merton, *Seven Storey Mountain* (New York: Garden City Books, 1951), 171–175.

[7] Merton, *Thoughts in Solitude*, 69.

2. The Elusive God of Hebrew Scriptures

[1] All citations from the Bible are from *The New Revised Standard Version Bible*, 1989.

[2] Richard Elliot Friedman, *The Hidden Face of God* (San Francisco: Harper SanFrancisco, 1995). This book was originally published as *The Disappearance of God*.

4. God of the Theologians

[1] Jaroslav Pelikan, *Jesus through the Centuries* (New Haven: Yale University Press, 1999), 58.

[2] See William Placher, *A History of Christian Theology: An Introduction* (Philadelphia: Westminster, 1983), 95.

[3] Denys Turner, *The Darkness of God: Negativity in Christian Mysticism* (New York: Cambridge University Press, 1995), 20.

⁴ Oliver Davies and Denys Turner, *Silence and the Word: Negative Theology and the Incarnation* (New York: Cambridge University Press, 2002).

⁵ See Placher, *History of Christian Theology*, 95−97, for a good summary of negative theology.

⁶ Augustine, *Confessions* (New York: Oxford University Press, 1992), 4−5.

⁷ Thomas Aquinas, *Summa Theologiae*, trans. Timothy McDermott, 1a,3, prologue, vol. 2 (London: Blackfriars, 1964), 19.

⁸ Paul Tillich, *Systematic Theology*, vol. I (Chicago: University of Chicago Press, 1957), 211−218.

⁹ Karl Rahner, *The Experience of Self and Experience of God*, in *Theological Investigations*, vol. 13 (New York: Seabury Press, 1975), 122−132.

¹⁰ Simone Weil, *Waiting for God*, trans. Emma Crauford (New York: Harper, 1951), 64.

5. God of the Mystics

¹ *Hadewijch: The Complete Works*, trans. Mother Columba Hart (New York: Paulist Press, 1980), quoted in *Medieval Women's Visionary Literature*, ed. Elizabeth Alvilda Petroff (New York: Oxford, 1986), 195−196.

² Bernard McGinn, *The Presence of God: A History of Western Mysticism*, vol. 3 (New York: Crossroad, 1998), 27.

³ Bonaventure, *The Triple Way* in *The Works of St. Bonaventure, I*, trans. Jose de Vinck (Paterson, NJ: St. Anthony Guild Press, 1960), 59−94.

⁴ Anonymous, *The Cloud of Unknowing*, introduction and translation by Ira Progoff (New York: Julian Press, 1969).

⁵ Meister Eckhart, *Meister Eckhart*, trans. Raymond Blakney (New York: Harper and Row, 1941), 227−230.

⁶ Ibid., 233.

⁷ Gerald Brennan, *St. John of the Cross: His Life and Poetry* (New York: Cambridge University Press, 1973).

⁸ For a superb exposition of these stages see Sandra Schneiders, *Finding the Treasure* (New York: Paulist Press, 2000), 159−182.

⁹ Mechthild of Magdeburg, *The Flowing Light of the Godhead* (New York: Paulist Press, 1998).

6. Tracking the Elusive God Today

¹ For a useful discussion of mystery see Paul Tillich, *Systematic Theology*, vol. 1 (Chicago: University of Chicago Press, 1951), 108−111.

² Carlo Ginzburg, *Wooden Eyes*, trans. Martin Ryle and Kate Soper (New York: Columbia University Press, 2001), offers some useful insights into the importance of making the familiar unfamiliar.

³ Nancy Mairs, *Ordinary Time: Cycles in Marriage, Faith, and Renewal* (Boston: Beacon, 1993), 11–12.

⁴ Annie Dillard, "An Expedition to the Pole," in *Teaching a Stone to Talk* (New York: Harper and Row, 1982). See also "Total Eclipse," 84–103.

⁵ Eckhart Tolle, *The Power of Now* (Novato, CA: New World Library, 1999), 11.

⁶ Alfred North Whitehead, *Religion in the Making* (New York: Macmillan, 1960), 74–75.

7. The Problem of Naming God

¹ For a good example of the influence of culture on images of Jesus see Jaroslav Pelikan's *Jesus through the Centuries* (New Haven: Yale University Press, 1999).

² Martin Buber, *I and Thou*, trans. Walter Kaufmann (New York: Charles Scribner's Sons, 1970).

8. God as Challenging Companion

¹ Karl Shapiro, "The 151st Psalm," in *Telling and Remembering: A Century of American Jewish Poetry*, ed. Steven Rubin (Boston: Beacon Press, 1999).

² Martha Manning, *A Place to Land: Lost and Found in an Unlikely Friendship* (New York: Random House, 2003).

9. God as Compassionate Adversary

¹ Simone Weil, *Waiting for God* (New York: Harper and Row, 1951), 69.

² Gerard Manley Hopkins, *Poems and Prose* (New York: Penguin, 1963), 67.

³ Kathy Hepinstall, *The House of Gentle Men* (New York: William Morrow, 2000), 311.

⁴ Stanley Weintraub, *Silent Night: The Story of the World War I Christmas Truce* (New York: Free Press, 2001).

10. God as Fertile Emptiness

¹ *Zen Flesh, Zen Bones: A Collection of Zen and Pre-Zen Writings*, compiled by Paul Reps (New York: Anchor, 1989), 5.

² Annie Dillard, *Teaching a Stone to Talk* (New York: Harper, 1982), 132–138.

³ *The Essential Rumi*, trans. Coleman Barks with John Moyne (New York: HarperSanFrancisco, 1955), 17.

⁴ *Meister Eckhart*, ed. Raymond Blakney (New York: Harper and Row, 1941), 230–231.
⁵ Ibid., 169.
⁶ Doris Grumbach, *The Presence of Absence* (Boston: Beacon, 1998).
⁷ T. S. Eliot, *Four Quartets* (New York: Harcourt, Brace, and World, 1943).
⁸ Lyndall Gordon, *Eliot's New Life* (New York: Farrar, Straus and Giroux, 1988), 108.

11. *New Challenges, New Spiritual Skills*

¹ Julie Salamon, *Rambam's Ladder: A Meditation on Generosity and Why It Is Necessary to Give* (New York: Workman, 2003).
² Henry David Thoreau, *A Writer's Journal* (New York: Dover, 1960), 93–94.
³ Natalia Ginzburg, *The Little Virtues*, trans. Dick Davis (New York: Seaver, 1986).

12. *Cultivating Skills of Radical Faith*

¹ Kathleen Norris, *Dakota: A Spiritual Geography* (New York: Houghton Mifflin, 1993).
² Fenton Johnson, *Keeping Faith: A Skeptic's Journey* (Boston: Houghton Mifflin, 2003).
³ For the results of her work on this project see Diana Eck, *A New Religious America* (New York: HarperSanFrancisco, 2001). For a personal account of her religious exploration see *Encountering God: A Spiritual Journey from Bozeman to Benares* (Boston: Beacon, 1993).
⁴ John Dunne, *The Way of All the Earth* (New York: Macmillan, 1972).
⁵ Denise Levertov, "The Work that Enfaiths," in *New and Selected Essays* (New York: New Directions, 1992), 247–257.
⁶ Flannery O'Connor, from *The Habit of Being*, quoted in *Wise Women*, ed. Susan Cahill (New York: Norton, 1996), 232–234.
⁷ Weil, *Waiting for God*, 99.

13. *Cultivating Skills of Contemplation*

¹ Sandra Schneiders, *Finding the Treasure: Locating Catholic Religious Life in a New Ecclesial and Cultural Context*, Religious Life in a New Millennium, vol. 1 (New York: Paulist, 2000), 159–160.
² Jane Kenyon, *A Hundred White Daffodils* (St. Paul: Graywolf Press, 1999).
³ Richard Foster, *Freedom of Simplicity* (New York: Harper and Row, 1989).

⁴ Robert Barron uses this story to illustrate the need to lay aside instruments of the ego when seeking to encounter God. See *And Now I See . . . : A Theology of Transformation* (New York: Crossroad, 1998), 93–101.

⁵ Mark Salzman, *Lying Awake* (New York: Alfred Knopf, 2000).

14. Cultivating Skills of Self-Knowledge

¹ Daniel Goleman, *Emotional Intelligence* (New York: Bantam, 1995), 54, 47.

² Robert Coles, *Lives of Moral Leadership* (New York: Random House, 2000), 22–151.

³ Roger Kamenetz, *The Jew in the Lotus: A Poet's Rediscovery of Jewish Identity in Buddhist India* (New York: HarperSanFrancisco, 1994), 125.

⁴ Gregory Orr, *The Blessing* (San Francisco: Council Oak Books, 2002).

⁵ Erich Fromm, *The Art of Loving* (New York: Harper and Row, 1956), 24.

⁶ Samuel Oliner, *Restless Memories: Recollections of the Holocaust Years* (Berkeley, CA: Judah L. Magness Memorial Museum, 1979). See also Morton Hunt, *The Compassionate Beast: What Science Is Discovering about the Human Side of Humankind* (New York: Morrow, 1990), which provides an account of Oliner's later development.

15. Awakening to a Hidden God

¹ T. S. Eliot, *Four Quartets* (New York: Harcourt, Brace, and World, 1943), 58–59.

² Thomas Merton, *The Asian Journal of Thomas Merton* (New York: New Directions, 1968), 233–234.

Index